"This study guide for Christian congregations is an excellent resource to help participants connect faith, personal health, and social responsibility to benefit self and to contribute to community and society well-being. Physical health, mental health, and spiritual health are linked to justice and social action, with Jesus as the model of community service and social change. Christian faith is brought to life through prayer, scripture, guided discussions, sharing of stories, dialogue, and interactive learning activities.

The guide integrates both religious readings from the Bible and scientific evidence that allows leaders to adapt the material to the unique needs of diverse congregations and participants. Sessions balance structure and flexibility in issues of time commitment, organizational format, content, and activities. Learning may be experienced through individual study and reflection, through group participation, or take-home activities. Specific examples incorporated throughout the study guide motivate participants to reach to their faith community and beyond by taking action locally and globally in social justice issues such as poverty, hunger, war and peace, and environmental stewardship.

I highly recommended this study guide for transforming Christians to make a difference in their own lives, their faith community, and society at large. The authors' integration of personal and social well-being is outstanding. In my role as reviewer, I have reexamined my own personal integration of physical, mental, and spiritual health. I have been motivated to recommit in acting on my faith to contribute more fully to the well-being of my faith community and to be a more engaged faithful steward within my local and global community."

Dennis T. Haynes, MSW, PhD
Professor and Chair, Department of Social Work,
University of Texas at San Antonio

Health Through Faith and Community

*A Study Resource
for Christian Faith Communities
to Promote Personal and Social Well-Being*

THE HAWORTH PASTORAL PRESS®
Rev. James W. Ellor, DMin, DCSW, CGP
Melvin A. Kimble, PhD
Co-Editors in Chief

Aging and Spirituality: Spiritual Dimensions of Aging Theory, Research, Practice, and Policy edited by David O. Moberg

Wu Wei, *Negativity, and Depression: The Principle of Non-Trying in the Practice of Pastoral Care* by Siroj Sorajjakool

Pastoral Care to Muslims: Building Bridges by Neville A. Kirkwood

Health Through Faith and Community: A Study Resource for Christian Communities to Promote Personal and Social Well-Being by Edward R. Canda, Aaron Ketchell, Phillip Dybicz, Loretta Pyles, and Holly Nelson-Becker

Spiritual Wisdom for Successful Retirement: Living Forward by C. W. Brister

Health Through Faith and Community

A Study Resource
for Christian Faith Communities
to Promote Personal and Social Well-Being

Edward R. Canda
Aaron Ketchell
Phillip Dybicz
Loretta Pyles
Holly Nelson-Becker

The Haworth Pastoral Press®
An Imprint of The Haworth Press, Inc.
New York • London • Oxford

For more information on this book or to order, visit
http://www.haworthpress.com/store/product.asp?sku=5595

or call 1-800-HAWORTH (800-429-6784) in the United States and Canada
or (607) 722-5857 outside the United States and Canada

or contact orders@HaworthPress.com

Published by

The Haworth Pastoral Press®, an imprint of The Haworth Press, Inc., 10 Alice Street, Binghamton, NY 13904-1580.

PUBLISHER'S NOTE
The development, preparation, and publication of this work has been undertaken with great care. However, the Publisher, employees, editors, and agents of The Haworth Press are not responsible for any errors contained herein or for consequences that may ensue from use of materials or information contained in this work. The Haworth Press is committed to the dissemination of ideas and information according to the highest standards of intellectual freedom and the free exchange of ideas. Statements made and opinions expressed in this publication do not necessarily reflect the views of the Publisher, Directors, management, or staff of The Haworth Press, Inc., or an endorsement by them.

This book provides educational information and opportunities for reflection about possible connections between faith and health of individuals and society. It is not intended as medical advice.

The United Methodist Health Ministry Fund grants permission for users of this book to photocopy pages for use as a learning resource.

Biblical quotes marked (NRSV) are taken from the New Revised Standard Version Bible, copyright 1989, Division of Christian Education of the National Council of the Churches of Christ in the United States of America. Used by permission. All rights reserved.

Scripture quotations marked (NIV) are taken from the HOLY BIBLE, NEW INTERNATIONAL VERSION®. Copyright © 1973, 1978, 1984 by International Bible Society. Used by permission of Zondervan. All rights reserved.

Cover design by Kerry E. Mack.

Library of Congress Cataloging-in-Publication Data

Health through faith and community : a study resource for Christian faith communities to promote personal and social well-being / Edward R. Canda . . . [et al.].
    p. cm.
  Includes bibliographical references and index.
  ISBN-13: 978-0-7890-2897-6 (soft : alk. paper)
  ISBN-10: 0-7890-2897-2 (soft : alk. paper)
  1. Health—Religious aspects—Christianity—Study and teaching. I. Canda, Edward R.
BT732.H44 2006
261.8'321—dc22

2005037979

CONTENTS

Acknowledgments

This study resource was developed by the Health Through Faith and Community Project, funded by the United Methodist Health Ministry Fund (UMHMF) of Hutchinson, Kansas. The Board of Trustees of the UMHMF conceived of this project to heighten awareness of social and spiritual factors that promote health for individuals and communities. UMHMF is dedicated to the extension of health, healing, and wholeness to all people. UMHMF Advisory Board, staff, and consultants encouraged this work.

Many thanks to the Advisory Committee for the Health Through Faith and Community Project, which has volunteered significant amounts of time and insight. Advisory Committee members have included the following:

R. Andrew Allison
Reverend Joe Babb
Mary Clarke Barkley
Reverend Cheryl J. Bell
Steve Coen
Jane Cooper
Debora Cox
Virginia Elliott
Stephen B. Fawcett, PhD
Marci Gieswein, RN
George Joehnk
Jackie John
Linda Johnson
Rick Johnson
Jeffrey A. Levin
Sandra Matthaei
Kim Moore
Reverend Doug Morphis
Pilar Oates
Marsha Stranathan
Larry W. Tobias

The authors also thank additional project staff who contributed to the development of this study resource: Sharon Barfield, Kris D'atri, and Laura Taylor. We are also grateful to the more than fifty United Methodist clergy and lay congregants who gave helpful suggestions during focus group interview sessions and informal discussion groups.

Health Through Faith and Community
Published by The Haworth Press, Inc., 2006. All rights reserved.
doi:10.1300/5595_a

ABOUT THE AUTHORS

Edward R. Canda, PhD, is Professor and Chair of the PhD Program, School of Social Welfare, University of Kansas, Lawrence. He is also Director of the project on Health Through Faith and Community, funded by the United Methodist Health Ministry Fund of Hutchinson, Kansas. He has written more than 100 publications and has given more than 100 presentations, most dealing with the connections between spirituality, cultural diversity, social work, and health. Dr. Canda is the co-author of *Spiritual Diversity in Social Work Practice: The Heart of Helping,* editor of *Spirituality in Social Work: New Directions* (Haworth), and co-editor of *Transpersonal Perspectives on Spirituality in Social Work* (Haworth).

Aaron Ketchell, PhD, is a lecturer in the Department of Religious Studies, American Studies Program, and Humanities and Western Civilization Program at the University of Kansas in Lawrence. He has been published on religion and American culture in the *Council of Societies for the Study of Religion Bulletin,* the *Great Plains Quarterly,* and the *Journal of American Culture.*

Phillip Dybicz, LCSW, MSW, has worked for several years in social work settings and is a PhD candidate at the University of Kansas in Lawrence.

Loretta Pyles, MA, PhD, is Assistant Professor in the School of Social Work at Tulane University in New Orleans. Her research includes issues of domestic violence, cultural competency, spirituality, and community development in post–Katrina New Orleans.

Holly B. Nelson-Becker, PhD, is Assistant Professor and Hartford Faculty Scholar in the School of Social Welfare at the University of Kansas in Lawrence. She is Chair of the interest group on Religion, Spirituality, and Aging for the Gerontological Society of America, and is a consulting editor of *Social Work,* the official journal of the National Association of Social Workers (NASW).

Introduction

About the Study Guide

STUDY GUIDE PURPOSE AND OBJECTIVES

Purpose

The purpose of this study guide is to encourage Christian congregations to enhance the well-being of church members as well as the wider society. This study guide flows from a Christian view of health that encompasses physical, mental, social, and spiritual aspects of well-being. The connection between personal health and social responsibility in a life of faith is given particular attention. We hope that this study guide will be useful for Christians who share an ideal of well-being for themselves and all people.

Objectives

This study guide will enable participants to

1. enhance their understanding of personal and community well-being,
2. expand their knowledge of spiritual and social factors that support health,
3. reflect on the quality of their physical, mental, spiritual, and social well-being in relation to their lives of faith,
4. reflect on the interconnection between their responsibility for both personal and community well-being,
5. adopt attitudes and behaviors that promote their overall well-being in the context of their lives of faith, and
6. develop a plan of action for enhancing their contributions to the well-being of the church community, the local community, and the wider society and world.

DESIGN AND FORMAT

Audience

This study guide is designed for adult members of Christian congregations who wish to learn more about connections between faith and both personal and social well-being for the benefit of themselves and their communities.

Health Through Faith and Community
Published by The Haworth Press, Inc., 2006. All rights reserved.
doi:10.1300/5595_01

Flow of Topics

This study guide contains eight sessions arranged in a series, each one building on the other. The sessions begin with a widely embracing view of spirituality and health. Viewing the pursuit of well-being as a spiritual journey, they then focus on well-being in various personal and social aspects of one's life. Sessions are designed to promote well-being from the individual person to the larger society. Throughout the study guide, the connections between personal health and social well-being are explored. Each session stands on its own in order to be useful for new or occasional participants. However, the deepest learning will result from participation in all sessions because each builds on the previous.

The life of faith combined with growth through learning involves the weaving together of one's inner personal life with outer social action—the union of awareness with action. Therefore, the principles that direct this study guide harmonize the inward and outward aspects of spiritual growth.

Principles Directing the Study Guide Content

Each session includes the following elements:

- Intention: Each session begins with a prayer to reinforce the group's intention to learn together. In this way, one's personal commitment to learning is linked with the purposes of the study guide itself. Members can commit to help each other have a good learning experience. Accomplishments of previous sessions will be summarized both for review and to include newcomers.
- Information: Pertinent information is presented crisply, in laypersons' terms, to increase one's knowledge and to present topics for exploration. The study guide offers working definitions, concepts, and content. Members are then invited to apply the information to their personal and social activities. This helps people to link awareness with action.
- Inspiration: Material comes from relevant Christian sources, scriptures, personal stories, images, literature, poetry, art, and other materials. It is hoped that these will help inspire participants spiritually, intuitively, and emotionally to connect with the information. This will help participants to relate to ideas with their whole selves and to see the potential of these ideas at work in their daily lives. The learning should be transformational.
- Introspection: Moments of quiet and self-reflection and of discussion will help participants gain insight into how the material is relevant to their personal lives and growth. Some of these introspective activities can be done in a group setting and some can be done privately.
- Interaction: Each session includes time for guided discussion, sharing of stories, spontaneous dialogue, and interactive exercises. Members can learn from one another and support one another in considering implications of the lessons. The joining of introspection and group interaction makes for a lively learning experience.
- Integration: A holistic Christian perspective on faith and health will infuse the study guide. All aspects of people in their life situations will be addressed: physical, mental, spiritual, and social. Throughout all sessions, we will integrate both personal and social well-being into a life of faith.

In addition, each session concludes with reflections summarized by the leader and participants. Supplemental activities are offered to promote ways to learn more about nurturing well-being in oneself, one's relationships, and the larger community. Additional suggestions and resources are available online at the following Web site: http://www.healthfaithstudy.info/.

Finally, the study guide concludes with a session designed to help congregations to create goals that will promote personal health and social health in the church community, local community, nation, and world. Offered online at the Web site just mentioned are guidelines that assist participants in forming an action committee to pursue these goals. The Web site also links to an online Spiritual Diversity and Social Work Resource Center. The Resource Center provides numerous bibliographical resources, essays, Internet links, and a photo gallery that address connections between spirituality, health, and social service in Christian and other religious traditions. This Resource Center is dedicated to the promotion of respect, wisdom, skill, and cooperation among professional social workers and allied advocates around the world regarding diverse religious and nonreligious spiritual approaches to health, well-being, peace, and justice.

Study Guide Venues

This study guide consists of eight sessions, each focusing on one theme to allow some depth of learning in a brief meeting time period (about fifty minutes). In this way, sessions can fit into adult Sunday school contexts or other brief time periods. Each session includes additional learning activities for use in longer meeting time periods or by individuals for personal learning outside of a group meeting.

The study guide is written in a user-friendly way so that leaders can easily apply the material in classes and individuals can use it for independent study. Leaders can adapt each session to the interests and needs of particular groups and community characteristics (such as rural or urban). Leaders can also adapt sessions of particular interest for use in briefer time periods. Various options for activities are included in each session.

There are five main ways that the study guide can be applied.

For the basics:

1. *Within eight adult Sunday school class meetings or other meetings of about fifty minutes.* In this case, one session without supplemental activities can be accomplished in one meeting period. Supplemental activities can be done individually outside of class, if participants desire. Allow a few minutes extra time at the beginning of each session to get settled.

For more intensive learning:

2. *Within sixteen adult Sunday school class meetings of about fifty minutes.* One session can be expanded to two class periods by completing the main activities in one class and completing supplemental activities in the subsequent class. Allow a few minutes extra time at the beginning of each session to get settled.

3. *Within eight longer meetings of about ninety minutes.* One expanded session, including selected supplemental activities, can be accomplished within one meeting period of one and a half hours. Allow a few minutes extra time at the beginning of each session to get settled.

4. *Within retreat formats.* In this case, the sessions can be conducted in sequence, with break times as needed, over a period of one and a half to two days (using all sessions' basic material plus some supplemental activities) or three days (using all sessions with most supplemental activities).

For independent learning:

5. The study guide is written with instructions for leaders to apply sessions in group settings. However, individuals could also go through the sessions in a self-study process by adapting the instructions to their own interests.

Study Guide Format

The study guide seeks to engage participants with a mix of approaches to learning and interaction. Therefore, each session blends various learning approaches (such as factual information; self-assessment and reflection exercises; small group discussion and interaction exercises; suggested further reading; Internet resources; and supplemental activities). The following is a brief overview of the format of each session.

I. Title Page and Quotes

On the title page of each session will be a list of various biblical quotes pertaining to the topic. These quotes will always be in *italics*.

These quotes can be used in a number of ways. The leader can offer them during the opening moments of prayer as points of departure for the session. In addition, some activities may wrap up early or extend into the next activity's time slot, leaving the leader with a few minutes before the session's end. At such a time, the leader can turn to these quotes to spur a brief discussion concerning their wisdom. These quotes are always included on their own page(s) for ease in transferring them to an overhead transparency if desired.

II. Session Setup

Introductory pages for each session contain information that will help the leader prepare and present the session. "Time" indicates the overall timeframe for the session. Approximate time allotments needed for specific activities are written in parentheses by their descriptions. "Materials" provides a brief list of the items that will be needed for that session's activities. An overhead projector and transparencies are always listed as optional in the event a leader should desire to transform any of the individual sections (e.g., title page with quotes, opening prayer, questions to consider) into this format. "Intention" gives the overall goal of the session, and "Objectives" spells out the goal more specifically. "Learning activities" provides directions for the entire session.

After these introductory pages, more detailed instructions and resources (such as overheads, handouts, and questions for discussion) are provided, as discussed in the following sections.

III. Activities

The top of each activity lists the learning objective for that particular activity. All instructions for the leader are set off by bullets.

Time is allotted at the beginning of each session for prayer as the first activity. This is to help set the group's intention for learning and as a form of welcome. Prayers are provided with each lesson that fit the theme of that lesson. Leaders may choose among these prayers or have participants offer their own. Opening prayers have been placed on their own page for easy photocopying. Leaders may transfer the prayer to a transparency for the entire group to pray or simply photocopy it and have an individual lead the prayer for the group. As with many aspects of this study guide, such flexibility allows leaders to match their own particular style and group interests.

In most sessions alternative activities are recommended. In addition, there are supplemental activities that could be used for extended sessions, private study, or as a replacement for one of the recommended activities. The leader should review all activities available prior to a session. The leader can either decide which to use within a given meeting time or allow participants to choose. Be aware that allowing choice may require a period of time to reach agreement.

Any information that the leader will need to read aloud to the group will be *enclosed within a box*. Additional information is often provided that leaders may use for their own preparation or to summarize for the group as desired.

An activity may contain additional background information. This information, while not essential to the lesson, is provided to help the leader capture the spirit and goal of the lesson. As time permits, leaders may share this information with participants when desired.

Most activities end with some type of group discussion. Thus, there is often a section ending the activity titled Questions to Consider. These questions are a useful aid for beginning a group discussion. In addition, quotes are sometimes provided at the bottom of this page to help spur reflection.

IV. Summing Up

It is important to briefly review key insights at the end of each session. Hitting these highpoints serves to reinforce their impact and help anchor the knowledge learned in the session. Introductory and closing summaries are provided, to be used if desired. Otherwise, leaders should feel free to sum up the lesson in their own words.

V. References

The references are citations for material that was consulted in creating the session. If desired, leaders can draw from the additional recommended readings and resources on spirituality, faith, and health provided on our Web site at http://www.healthfaithstudy.info/.

Session 1

A Holistic Christian Vision of Health
Through Faith and Community

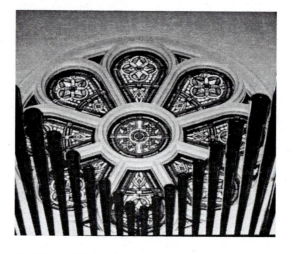

Stained-glass window, First United Methodist Church, Lawrence, Kansas. (All photos by authors.)

O Lord, by these things people live, and in all these is the life of my spirit. Oh, restore me to health and make me live!

Isaiah 38:16 (NRSV)

Pleasant words are a honeycomb, sweet to the soul and healing to the bones.

Proverbs 16:24 (NIV)

There is one whose rash words are like sword thrusts, but the tongue of the wise brings healing.

Proverbs 12:18 (NIV)

It is not the healthy who need a doctor, but the sick. But go and learn what this means: "I desire mercy, not sacrifice."

Matthew 9:12-13 (NIV)

Health Through Faith and Community
Published by The Haworth Press, Inc., 2006. All rights reserved.
doi:10.1300/5595_02

All the believers were one in heart and mind. No one claimed that any of his possessions was his own, but they shared everything they had. . . . There were no needy persons among them. For from time to time those who owned lands or houses sold them, brought the money from the sales and put it at the apostles' feet, and it was distributed to anyone as he had need.

Acts 4:32-35 (NIV)

Time: Fifty minutes plus optional fifty minutes for supplemental activities

Materials:

- Leader's Guide
- Pens/pencils/scratch paper
- Overhead projector
- Overhead transparencies and handouts

Intention: To provide participants with an introduction to the study guide and to a holistic Christian view of health through faith and community

Objectives: During this session, participants will

1. Learn about the overall purpose, organization, and format of the study guide
2. Agree to basic values for trust and mutual respect that are necessary for a successful and enjoyable learning experience
3. Gain a holistic view of health through faith and community
4. Identify some definitions of key terms related to faith and health used in this study guide
5. Begin exploring their own understandings of health in relation to their spiritual journeys

Learning Activities

Setting Intention Through Welcome and Prayer (five minutes)

- Introduce yourself briefly (if necessary). Briefly share your interest in the present topic.
- Welcome participants and encourage them to ask questions or contribute to discussions throughout the meetings.
- Ask for a moment of quiet and either offer a short prayer or invite a participant to offer one that sets an intention for participants to be open to learning and supporting each other. (See Activity 1 for suggested prayerful reflections.)

Introducing Themes Related to Session 1 (five minutes)

- Please read the following:

> Today's session will concentrate on familiarizing ourselves with the overall topic of this study guide and some of its key concepts.

- Read the following theme descriptions to introduce the topics explored in today's lesson.
- As this is the first lesson, inform the group that these activities will be done in order. Future lessons allow for your discretion or group input in choosing activities.

> *Activity 2—Explaining the Purpose and Overall Plan of the Study Guide*
> In this activity, we briefly look at the six aspects of this study guide: Intention, Information, Inspiration, Introspection, Interaction, and Integration.

Activity 3—Commitment to Mutual Respect and Dialogue
The purpose of this activity is for us to make an outward commitment to respect each other within the learning process.

Activity 4—Participants' Views on Health and Faith
In this activity, we will discuss our own views on what various aspects of health mean to each of us.

Activity 5—Preliminary Definitions Regarding Faith and Health
In this activity, we will compare our views from Activity 4 to sample definitions provided in order to extend discussion and create our own agreed on definitions for this study guide.

Group Activities and Discussion (about thirty-five minutes)

- Complete Activity 2 (about five minutes).
- Complete Activity 3 (about five minutes) and conduct a group discussion.
- Complete Activity 4 (about ten minutes) and conduct a group discussion.
- Complete Activity 5 (about fifteen minutes) and conduct a group discussion.

Concluding Reflections (five minutes)

- Ask participants for any concluding comments.
- Provide a summary and wrapup of the meeting (see Summing Up).
- Thank participants and inquire into the group's interest in the optional supplemental activities (to work on either independently or at next meeting).

Supplemental, In-Group, or Take-Home Activities (fifty minutes)

Unexplored themes can be used as supplemental activities, allowing extended time for discussion or reflection.

You and/or participants can use Supplemental Activities A through D for resources within an extended meeting time or for independent learning. Supplemental Activity A extends Activity 5 by allowing participants to reflect on what each of the key terms means to them. Supplemental Activity B (The Healing Ministry of Jesus) is useful as a source of inspiration when examining this study guide. The story in Supplemental Activity C can be read as the basis for a discussion about the ways Christian faith can promote strength in adversity. Supplemental Activity D can be used to increase one's own interpretation of key concepts related to faith and health and how they relate to personal belief and experience.

ACTIVITY 1:
SETTING INTENTION THROUGH WELCOME AND PRAYER

Time: Five minutes

Objective: To welcome participants and to set an intention for learning

- Introduce yourself briefly, including your interest in the present topic.
- Welcome participants and encourage them to ask questions or contribute to discussions throughout the meetings.
- Ask for a moment of quiet and either offer a short prayer or invite a participant to offer one that sets an intention for participants to be open to learning and supporting each other. If you are interested in suggestions for an opening prayer, two such prayers are provided.

OPENING PRAYER
(Suggestion 1)

Creator God, as we gather today
create in us the will to be open to new experiences
and the desire to hear deeply the words
each one shares.

Awaken in us a holy curiosity
that challenges our complacency
and moves us forward into new places
where we discover what it means
to develop and protect healthy bodies, spirits, relationships, and communities.
Help us hold the needs of all people
gently in our hands
as together we begin to build a community
sustained by love.

Finally, may the light of your love guide our path
as we learn to love each other and all people
more fully in this task.

We ask this in the name of Jesus Christ
by the Holy Spirit.

Amen.

OPENING PRAYER
(Suggestion 2)

Almighty God, thank Thee for the job of this day.
May we find gladness in all its toil and difficulty,
its pleasure and success,
and even in its failure and sorrow.

We would look always away from ourselves,
and behold the glory and the need of the world
that we may have the will and the strength to bring
the gift of gladness to others;
that with them we stand to bear
the burden and heat of the day
and offer Thee the praise of work well done.

Amen.

**Charles Lewis Slattery,
early twentieth-century
Episcopal bishop***

Note: All prayers in this study guide that are attributed to an individual author are taken from the Web site of The World Prayers Project. They state the following as their Web site's purpose: "The World Prayers Project (WPP) is a nonprofit, educational, public service organization whose founding objective is to gather and present historic and contemporary World Prayers in a unified, multifaith archive on the Internet." (http://www.worldprayers.org/)

ACTIVITY 2:
OVERVIEW OF THE STUDY GUIDE

Time: About five minutes

Objective: To understand how the study guide is set up to support learning

- Review the Preface to this study guide for background prior to the meeting.
- Please read the following:

> This study guide contains eight sessions arranged in a series, each one building on the other. This session begins by exploring a holistic, or widely embracing, view of faith and health. Future sessions will then focus on specific personal and social aspects of health, viewing them as part of one's spiritual journey. Sessions are designed to promote well-being from the individual person to the larger society. Throughout the study guide, the connections between personal health and social well-being are explored. Each session stands on its own in order to be useful for newcomers to the group. However, the deepest learning will result from participation in all sessions because each builds on the previous.
>
> The life of faith combined with growth through learning involves the weaving together of one's inner personal life with outer social action—the union of awareness with action. Therefore, the principles that direct the study guide harmonize the inward and outward aspects of spiritual growth.

- Display Overhead 1.1, which gives a synopsis of the study guide's principles. Feel free to elaborate by using the "Principles Directing the Study Guide Content" section in the Introduction.

OVERHEAD 1.1. Study guide's principles.

- *Intention:* Each session begins with a prayer to reinforce the group's intention to learn.
- *Information:* Pertinent information from spiritual, scholarly, and other sources is presented to increase knowledge and present topics for exploration.
- *Inspiration:* Material is included from pertinent Christian sources, scriptures, personal stories, and other materials as a way to inspire participants spiritually, intuitively, and emotionally.
- *Introspection:* Moments of quiet and self-reflection exercises are offered in order to help participants to be in touch with their inner responses to the material.
- *Interaction:* Each session includes time for discussion and interactive exercises so participants can learn from each other.
- *Integration:* A Christian perspective on faith and health will infuse the study guide and integrate many aspects of health.

ACTIVITY 3:
COMMITMENT TO MUTUAL RESPECT AND DIALOGUE

Time: About five minutes

Objective: To agree to values of mutual respect and dialogue to guide the learning experience

To promote enjoyable and effective learning, the group needs to make a commitment to values addressing mutual respect. Adapt the following values, as necessary, for discussion with the group.

- Please read the following:

> To engage in respectful dialogue, the following values are a helpful reference. The purpose of this activity is to adopt a set of agreed on values to guide our group. Let's agree to gently remind each other to maintain these values, and, if honest mistakes are made, let us support each other in correcting them.

- Display Overhead 1.2, which lists the values guiding the group.
- Use Questions to Consider as a prompt for brief discussion, leading to a group affirmation of the values.
- End the activity by asking the group for a sign of collective agreement with the final agreed on values, such as verbal assent or applause.

OVERHEAD 1.2. Values to guide our group.

Trust: To be open and honest, participants must be able to trust one another to keep these values within the sessions and after the sessions are completed. A sense of trust means that things said in confidence should remain in confidence.

Sincerity: All our communication should be honest and sincere. When we sense one another's sincerity, we will know that we have a real commitment to one another and the community.

Respect: We must treat one another with respect at all times, in both speech and action. No one should monopolize the time of the group. Everyone should have an equal opportunity to participate.

Willingness to learn: We need to be willing to learn, to increase our awareness of both our strengths and our limitations, and to work on issues at hand. Everyone is engaged in learning in different ways at different levels. It is a lifelong process. Let's support each other in our learning.

Agreement to disagree: Real maturity and respect in communication go beyond being comfortable with like-minded people. We need to acknowledge and respect differences and disagreements. If we agree to disagree, we can search for a common understanding that is deeper than the disagreement but that also respects our right to be different.

Commitment to work through issues: If disagreements or challenges arise, we need to be persistent in working them through. Otherwise, tension can develop and linger. Working through issues leads to insight and nurturing relationships.

Source: Adapted from Canda, Carrizosa, & Yellow Bird, 1995.

Questions to Consider

1. What questions or concerns do you have about these values?

2. What would you like to discuss that would help us reach agreement about these values?

ACTIVITY 4:
PARTICIPANTS' VIEWS ON FAITH AND HEALTH

Time: About ten minutes

Objective: To help participants to express their personal understandings of important terms used in these lessons

- Distribute the Questions to Consider on Handout 1.1, and ask participants to take a few minutes to answer them.
- Begin a *brief* discussion regarding these terms. (Note: Make sure you save a few minutes to conclude with Activity 5.)

HANDOUT 1.1. Questions to consider.

---

1. What do the terms "spirituality," "faith," and "religion" mean to you? Feel free to give examples.

2. How would you define "health" or "well-being"?

3. In your life experience, in what ways has fostering spirituality, faith, or religion affected the health of individuals and communities? Give a brief example.

ACTIVITY 5:
PRELIMINARY DEFINITIONS REGARDING FAITH AND HEALTH

Time: About fifteen minutes

Objective: To develop definitions for important terms used in these lessons

- Please read the following:

> For the purposes of this study guide, the authors are viewing health as the maintenance and nurturing of personal and social well-being. Maintenance refers to efforts of prevention and of avoiding illness or social problems. Nurturing refers to active efforts to support positive qualities of persons and communities. It also involves seeking change for the better. In addition, the authors are adopting a holistic view of health; this means a view of health that includes the following parts: physical, mental, social, and spiritual.

- Display Overhead 1.3, which summarizes the preliminary definitions. Feel free to elaborate by using the additional information supplied. If you wish to explain the following symbolism of the stained-glass window, you can distribute Handout 1.2.
- Emphasize that this is a brief introduction to these ideas and that they will be explored in more detail throughout the study guide.
- Also emphasize that these ideas are meant to stimulate participants to clarify their own understandings and definitions.
- Use Questions to Consider for Overhead 1.3 as prompts for discussion.

With regard to spirituality, we (the authors) will be emphasizing how the inner aspects of faith connect with the outward aspects of our lives in the church community and the wider society. We will be considering how spirituality impacts physical, mental, and social health. We will also be examining how social factors, such as the state of the economy and resources for all members of society, impact health of body, mind, spirit, and relationships. We hope that this study guide will support individuals and congregations in their spiritual journeys toward a sense of wholeness, well-being, peace, and justice.

Well-being depends on the nurturing of connections and interactions. It is a product of harmony among physical, mental, social, and spiritual areas of life. Just as spirituality, faith, and religion all necessitate a focus on human-divine and human-human relationships, someone seeking to foster his or her well-being must be able to think and act in a holistic or unitary fashion. While the journey toward health involves attention to one's inner relationship with God, progress in this direction also necessitates community support and responsibility. Therefore, this study guide calls for the recognition of vital linkages among individuals and their larger social environment.

The stained-glass window shown in the photograph at the beginning of this chapter provides a beautiful metaphor for a holistic view of health. The rose-like pattern of the window, with spokes reaching in all directions and unified in connection at the center, can represent the way that all areas of life must be harmonized and unified for well-being to flourish. The light shining through can represent the grace of God that gives support and insight to promote health of mind, body, spirit, and society. The pipes of the organ that surround the window can represent the intention to share the benefits of our own personal health by promoting the well-being of the wider society and world, like the wonderful music that spreads out from around the rose window. (Note: An enlarged version of this photo is included as Handout 1.3 in the event that you would like to share this metaphor with the participants.)

In this study guide, we view health as more than just the absence of symptoms of illness or even the presence of symptoms of health in any one area of life. Holistic well-being encourages physical, mental, social, and spiritual health. Even in the midst of illness or distress, we can continue to grow on the journey of faith toward well-being. All people experience difficulty, illness, and death at some point. The life of faith can bring well-being through the negative as well as the positive experiences in life, for individuals and for society.

Preliminary Definitions

Below, we offer some preliminary definitions of key terms as a starting point for reflection and discussion. They are not instructions for how you should define or think about these terms. We intend these to help you clarify your own understandings of these terms and what they mean in your lives.

overall well-being: A sense that a person has a general positive condition of life that results from harmonizing physical, mental, social, and spiritual areas. Qualities of well-being include inner peacefulness, the ability to cope well with challenges, responsible relationships, participation in the community, and attentiveness to growing in faith. As the story in Supplemental Activity B suggests, a person can develop a sense of well-being even during times of poor physical health.

physical health: A good condition and functioning of the body. Potential ills include the common cold, serious disease, and chronic high blood pressure. Qualities of physical health include physical vitality, healthy diet, balanced lifestyle, the ability to accomplish daily activities, and possession of good skills to address physical limitations.

mental health: Peace of mind, clear thinking, and emotional balance. Potential ills include distress, depression, anxiety, and serious psychiatric disorders. Qualities of mental health include good self-esteem, good problem-solving skills, enthusiasm, and an ability to enjoy life.

social health: Well-being of one's community and society and one's relationship to them as an active member. Potential ills include poverty, crime, and alienation. Qualities of social health include peace, justice, mutual care, and provision for needs of all members of society.

spiritual health: Heightened awareness of one's spirituality and ongoing spiritual growth. Potential ills include self-absorption, apathy, sin, and a sense of meaninglessness. Qualities of spiritual health include a positive sense of humility, thankfulness, and connection with oneself, other people, the universe, and God.

faith: A belief and trust in God and awareness of God's loving presence in the world. This can act as a source of daily insight and encouragement and as a base for strength and hope in times of difficulty.

religion: A formally organized institutional framework of beliefs, values, and practices for remembering, honoring, and growing in faith through both public and private expressions.

spirituality: A way of exploring and developing the deep meaning, purpose, and values of life in relationship to ourselves, others, and God. This yields a commitment to live responsibly and lovingly in relation to loved ones, other people, communities, and the world. For most Americans, spirituality includes a life of faith and participation in religious groups.

All of these terms imply

1. a reliance on *relationships* (personal and communal);
2. a *journey* or *process* of life and faith;
3. *interconnection* of person, society, world, and God; and
4. *balance and harmony* between different aspects of well-being.

OVERHEAD 1.3.
Preliminary definitions.

overall well-being: A sense that a person has a general positive condition of life that results from harmonizing the physical, mental, social, and spiritual areas of one's life.

physical health: A good condition and functioning of the body such as physical vitality, healthy diet, balanced lifestyle, ability to accomplish daily activities, and possession of good skills to address physical limitations.

mental health: Peace of mind, clear thinking, and emotional balance.

social health: Well-being of one's community and society and one's relationship to them as an active member.

spiritual health: Heightened awareness of one's spirituality and ongoing spiritual growth.

faith: A belief and trust in God and awareness of God's loving presence in the world. This can act as a source of daily insight and encouragement and as a base for strength and hope in times of difficulty.

religion: A formally organized institutional framework of beliefs, values, and practices for remembering, honoring, and growing in faith through both public and private expressions.

spirituality: A way of exploring and developing the deep meaning, purpose, and values of life in relationship to ourselves, others, and God. This yields a commitment to live responsibly and lovingly in relation to loved ones, other people, communities, and the world. For most Americans, this includes a life of faith and participation in religious groups.

All of these terms imply

1. a reliance on *relationships* (personal and communal);
2. a *journey* or *process* of life and faith;
3. *interconnection* of person, society, world, and God; and
4. *balance and harmony* between different aspects of well-being.

Questions to Consider

1. In what ways do the preliminary definitions match your own ideas that you reflected on earlier?

2. What, if anything, do you feel needs to be added to or subtracted from these definitions?

HANDOUT 1.2. Stained-glass window, First United Methodist Church, Lawrence, Kansas.

Stained-glass window, First United Methodist Church, Lawrence, Kansas.

SUMMING UP

Objective: To summarize what was learned in today's lesson

- You may use the following as guides for summarizing today's lesson:

> Today we learned a little about what this study guide has to offer, and we have made a commitment in our approach to learning.

- Read the following:

Overview of the Study Guide

> In Activity 1, we read about the six "I"s: Intention, Information, Inspiration, Introspection, Interaction, and Integration. These all combine together in a effort to make this a rich learning experience for everyone.

Commitment to Mutual Respect and Dialogue

> In Activity 2, we discussed the values that should guide our group, and we made a commitment to follow these values while pursing our learning.

Views on Faith and Health

> Finally, in Activity 3, we explored some key concepts and what they each mean for us. Some noteworthy comments from this discussion were. . . . [Use specific examples from the discussion.]

- Conclude with the following:

Conclusion

> Our explorations today were a brief introduction to concepts of well-being. For those who have an interest in further exploration, feel free to examine the supplemental activities at the end of this session.

- Note: Those who wish to explore any lessons independently will need copies of the directions from the Leader's Guide.

SUPPLEMENTAL ACTIVITY A:
EXPLORING PERSONAL DEFINITIONS
OF SPIRITUALITY AND HEALTH

Time: Ten minutes

Objective: To reflect on what the terms discussed in Activity 5 personally mean to you

- Distribute Handout 1.3 (Personal Definitions) to participants interested in creating their own definitions upon returning home.

HANDOUT 1.3. Personal definitions.

This exercise is for those who would like to think in more detail about the terms related to health and spirituality. Please briefly describe what the following terms mean *to you* when you hear them or use them. Jot down brief words or phrases rather than full sentences. If any of these terms are not significantly different from the preliminary definitions provided, feel free to leave that section blank.

Spirituality:

Faith:

Religion:

Physical health:

Mental health:

Social health:

Spiritual health:

Overall well-being:

SUPPLEMENTAL ACTIVITY B:
THE HEALING MINISTRY OF JESUS

Time: Twenty minutes

Objective: To draw inspiration from the healing ministry of Jesus

- Allow time for participants to read Handout 1.4 (Jesus' Healing Ministry) or read it aloud.
- Then use Questions to Consider for Handout 1.4 as prompts for discussion.

HANDOUT 1.4. Jesus' healing ministry.

The examples of Jesus' healing ministry given in the gospels constitute four modes of healing: physical, mental, spiritual, and social. These four modes serve as a source of inspiration for this study guide.

The Gospel of Mark has several references to *physical* healing in its first chapter. Jesus healed the man with the unclean spirit (Mark 1:23-26), leaving the scribes amazed at the power of his authority. Next he healed Simon's mother-in-law of fever (30-31). Her first action after this healing was to serve Jesus and the apostles. Next, at sundown, people from the city arrived and he healed many who were sick with various diseases as well as cast demons out (32-34). Jesus healed a leper and a man who was paralyzed (40-42; 2:3-12). This healing ministry was a central part of Jesus' message and is repeated in all the Gospels.

The stories told in Mark of the unclean spirit and casting out of demons are examples of restoring *mental* health. Other examples that display this emphasis include Jesus' removal of evil spirits from Mary Magdalene (Luke 8:2) and his healing of the Gerasene Demoniac (Mark 5:1-20). In the latter account, a man possessed by so many demons that even shackles and chains could not subdue him achieved his "right mind" after Jesus ordered the spirits to depart.

Spiritual healing connotes the atonement aspect of his ministry. The atonement or at-one-ment is the holistic relating of being to the world at large: this is our place, made for us, or, as the scientist might say, we have our ecological niche in the universe. We are part of an entire system of life and being. Jesus demonstrated such atonement in Luke 19:2-9. In this passage, he lodged with the tax collector, Zacchaeus, despite the fact that onlookers believed him to be a sinner. As a result of this act, Zacchaeus agreed to give charitable contributions to the poor and to end his fraudulent ways—transformations that Jesus claimed would lead to his salvation.

As Christ came into the world to reconcile humanity to God, that reconciliation includes breaking down our separateness from the world and promoting *social* health. That separation is something we have created through sin, and Christ's role is to restore us to wholeness by (1) creating the doorway to salvation by his crucifixion and resurrection and by (2) demonstrating God's love and unity by overcoming barriers of race, class, and all other distinctions.

Jesus' philosophy of sympathy and kindness is best expressed through the Beatitudes. By blessing "the poor in spirit," "those who mourn," "the meek," "those who hunger and thirst for righteousness," "the merciful," "the pure in heart," "the peacemakers," and "those who are persecuted for righteousness' sake" (Matthew 5:4-10), he demonstrated a concern for social well-being that pervades the Gospels. While transforming the physical, mental, and spiritual aspects of individuals' health, his ministry to the oppressed and subjugated offers a model for the establishment of the Kingdom of God on Earth. Another example of the accentuation of social health can be found in Matthew 25:34-36, when Jesus stated, "'Come you that are blessed by my Father, inherit the kingdom prepared for you from the foundation of the world; for I was hungry and you gave me food, I was thirsty and you gave me something to drink, I was a stranger and you welcomed me, I was naked and you gave me clothing, I was sick and you took care of me, I was in prison and you visited me.'"

Jesus most commonly healed through words or touch. Healing sometimes occurred when individuals touched him or his clothes, and sometimes the faith of the individuals seemed to be a factor in the healing. Healing occurred on several occasions when Jesus had compassion for people and then proceeded to actively heal them. In fact, the reason he most often healed is be-

Note: All biblical citations are taken from the New Revised Standard Version of the Bible.

cause he cared deeply about people. He loved them and so he healed them. Healing was a natural result of the person he was, both divine and human.

The ministry of Jesus included preaching, teaching, and healing. Therefore, Jesus is today referred to as the Great Physician. Even the adversaries of Jesus did not question the healing power he exerted. Nearly one-fifth of the Gospels are devoted to Jesus' acts of healing (Kelsey, 1987). In fact, his healing ministry was presented as evidence that he was the Messiah: "Go and tell John what you hear and see: the blind receive their sight, the lame walk, the lepers are cleansed, the deaf hear, the dead are brought to life" (Matthew 11:4-5).

Questions to Consider for Handout 1.4

1. In what ways do you feel that you have been able in the past to draw on the healing power of Jesus?

2. How does the healing aspect of Christ's ministry extend your understanding of both personal and social health?

SUPPLEMENTAL ACTIVITY C:
A STORY OF HEALTH THROUGH FAITH

Time: Fifteen minutes

Objective: To draw inspiration from one individual's story of health through faith

- Allow time for participants to read Handout 1.5 (Joan's Story) or read it aloud. Feel free to elaborate on this story by using the additional information provided in the following paragraphs.
- Use Questions to Consider for Handout 1.5 as prompts for discussion.

People can develop a sense of well-being even while dealing with adversity. For example, some people draw on their faith in order to grow in awareness of life's meaning. They use illness as an opportunity rather than an obstacle. They learn how spirituality and faith are interwoven with health and well-being. The physical, mental, social, and spiritual challenges of illness present clear choices. Those who choose to approach illness as an opportunity for learning offer us valuable lessons. A life of faith can foster well-being even when physical abilities decline.

In a study of adults who have the chronic illness called cystic fibrosis (a hereditary life-threatening condition) it was found that some people were able to strengthen their well-being through personal and community prayer, support from faith community members, and a deep sense of relationship with a loving God (Canda, 2001, 2002). By relying on faith as a sacred source of strength, they described their ability to find meaning through illness and to go beyond the limitations of the body. They stressed how important it is for everyone to treasure each moment, to cherish loved ones, to grow spiritually, and to use their own situations to help and inspire others. The story of Joan illustrates this.

HANDOUT 1.5. Joan's story.

Joan, in her thirties, has always lived with cystic fibrosis. She considers her personal relationship with God and Jesus as the most important part of her life. Her family, friends, and congregation actively supported her with prayer and loving helpfulness. When Joan and her husband were awaiting a transplant to replace her severely damaged lungs, she was so sick and weak that she actually gave up attachment to life. Yet in the midst of this she vividly felt the intimate presence of God comforting and supporting her like a "circle of protection." Even in the face of immense anxiety, she felt that God sent an angel-like presence to protect her through the danger and difficulty of a lung transplant.

The awareness of a sacred circle of protection prompted a series of dreams as symbols of the divine powers supporting her. In one dream, Joan was extremely sick and shivered from a cold, strong wind bombarding her. Suddenly, she felt the strong, gentle hand of an angel named Michael. The angel and her husband held her so that she would not be blown away. Then the angel helped her and her husband don rain gear symbolic of protection for the time ahead.

Joan felt this angelic presence encircle, protect, and comfort her throughout the stresses of her sickness and surgery. Even during the pain and grueling treatments, Joan felt a source of supernatural strength. Joan felt very clearly that even if she died on the operating table, she would be all right within the loving embrace of God. When the transplant was over Joan was exhausted. Yet, she also felt born into a new opportunity for an ongoing life of faith and service to other people.

This sense of a circle of protection remained after the transplant. A few times, even years later, Joan would feel a warm sense of joy in her chest that lasted all day. Even Joan thought it sounded odd, but she was certain of the feeling. She said it was as if the Holy Spirit was within her.

Since the transplant Joan has enjoyed greatly improved physical health. However, with greater physical strength, she also has experienced temptations to be distracted from her spiritual commitments. Joan said that she has to remind herself to stay on the path of faith during the good times as well as the bad. She has not felt the intense angelic presence lately but knows for a certainty that God is with her. With a new perspective on life, Joan is not afraid of any physical ailments and knows that this deep sense of connectedness with God will always be with her.

Source: Story adapted from Canda, 2001, 2002.

Questions to Consider for Handout 1.5

1. In what ways did Joan's Christian faith help her to experience well-being even in the midst of serious illness and the risk of death?

2. Have you or someone you know experienced a similar sense of well-being during a time of adversity? Please describe.

SUPPLEMENTAL ACTIVITY D: ENVISIONING YOUR IDEAL OF WELL-BEING

Time: Five minutes

Objective: An opportunity to exercise your creativity regarding health and well-being

If you wish, take a moment to relax, clear your mind, and center yourself. Then, please jot down any words, images, metaphors, or drawings that represent your *overall ideal of health and well-being.*

Session 2

Faith and Physical Health

Stained-glass window, Clarice L. Osborne Memorial Chapel (Baker University, Baldwin City, Kansas) reading "I was sick and ye visited me"—Matthew 25:36 (KJV).

For I will restore health to you, and your wounds I will heal, says the Lord.

Jeremiah 30:17 (NRSV)

If you will listen carefully to the voice of the Lord your God, and do what is right in his sight, and give heed to his commandments and keep all his statutes, I will not bring upon you any diseases . . . for I am the Lord who heals you.

Exodus 15:26 (NRSV)

Health Through Faith and Community
Published by The Haworth Press, Inc., 2006. All rights reserved.
doi:10.1300/5595_03

Are any among you sick? They should call for the elders of the church and have them pray over them, anointing them with oil in the name of the Lord . . . pray for one another, so that you may be healed. The prayer of the righteous is powerful and effective.

James 5:14, 16 (NRSV)

Then he [Jesus] returned from the region of Tyre, and went by way of Sidon toward the Sea of Galilee, in the region of the Decapolis. They brought to him a deaf man who had an impediment in his speech; and they begged him to lay his hand on him. He took him aside in private, away from the crowd and put his fingers into his ears, and he spat and touched his tongue. Then looking up to heaven, he sighed and said to him, "Ephphatha," that is, "Be opened." And immediately his tongue was released, and he spoke plainly. . . . They were astounded beyond measure, saying, "He has done everything well; he even makes the deaf to hear and the mute to speak."

Mark 7:31-37 (NRSV)

Time: Fifty minutes plus optional fifty minutes for supplemental activities

Materials:

- Leader's Guide
- Pens/pencils/scratch paper
- Overhead projector
- Overhead transparencies and handouts
- Pitcher of water, large bowl, towels (Supplemental Activity B)

Intention: To introduce participants to issues concerning the relationships among religious participation, faith, and physical health

Objectives: During this session, participants will

1. Discuss ways in which faith and physical health currently complement each other in one's own life.
2. Explore new ways in which faith can be drawn on to enrich one's physical health.
3. Examine how the interaction between physical health and faith can offer a bridge toward empathizing with the health of one's community and those who suffer within it.

Learning Activities:

Setting Intention Through Welcome and Prayer (five minutes)

- Introduce yourself briefly (if necessary). Briefly share your interest in the present topic.
- Welcome participants and encourage them to ask questions or contribute to discussions throughout the meetings.
- Summarize the accomplishments from previous sessions. The following paragraph may be used for this purpose. Adapt it according to the activities completed.

> The first session of this study guide encouraged us to develop a view of health in relation to Christian faith. We learned about the overall purpose, organization, and format of the study guide. We agreed to basic values for trust and mutual respect, examined the definition of "holistic health" and other key terms, and began to explore our own understandings of health and spirituality.

- Ask for a moment of quiet and either offer a short prayer or invite a participant to offer one that sets an intention for participants to be open to learning and supporting each other. (See Activity 1 for suggested prayerful reflections.)

Introducing Themes Related to Session 2 (five minutes)

- Please read the following:

> Today's session will concentrate on familiarizing ourselves with the relationships among faith, religion, and physical health.

- If you have chosen ahead of time one or two of the following activities for this session, read the appropriate descriptions (feel free to choose one of the supplemental activities as a main activity if you feel it best suits your group's needs).
- If you wish to allow time to let the group choose the activities for today's session, read the activity descriptions below to introduce possible topics for exploration in today's lesson. Allow the group to choose one or two of the activities for completion during today's session.

Activity 2—Finding Meaning Through Suffering (about fifteen to twenty minutes)
In this activity, we examine the role of religious belief in dealing with illness or disability and explore one's ability to empathize with another's suffering.

Activity 3—Exercise and Prayerfulness (about fifteen to twenty minutes)
In this activity, we examine ways that physical activity can combine with prayer.

Activity 4—Religious Participation As It Relates to a Healthy Lifestyle (about fifteen to twenty minutes)
In this activity, we examine how religious participation helps individuals avoid risk behaviors and maintain healthy lifestyles.

Group Activities and Discussion (about thirty-five to forty minutes)

- Begin the first chosen activity and conduct a group discussion. Prompts for group discussion are included in the activities in Questions to Consider.
- If time allows, begin the second chosen activity.

Concluding Reflections (five minutes)

- Ask participants for any concluding comments.
- Provide a summary and wrap-up of the meeting (see Summing Up).
- Thank participants and inquire into the group's interest in the optional supplemental activities (to work on either independently or at the next meeting).

Supplemental, In-Group, or Take-Home Activities (fifty minutes)

Remaining themes can be used as supplemental activities, allowing extended time for discussion or reflection.

You and/or participants can use Supplemental Activities A through C for resources within an extended meeting time or for independent learning. Supplemental Activity A explores healing prayers and suggests how mental imagery may be a useful tool for this practice. Supplemental Activity B explores ceremony as a way to instill faith into one's healing process or maintenance of well-being. Supplemental Activity C extends Activity 2 (Finding Meaning Through Suffering) by exploring the practice of fasting and how this may help one to empathize with those who suffer from hunger.

ACTIVITY 1:
SETTING INTENTION
THROUGH WELCOME AND PRAYER

Time: Five minutes

Objective: To welcome participants and to set an intention for learning

- Introduce yourself briefly, including your interest in the present topic.
- Welcome participants and encourage them to ask questions or contribute to discussions throughout the meetings.
- Ask for a moment of quiet and either offer a short prayer or invite a participant to offer one that sets an intention for participants to be open to learning and supporting each other. If you are interested in suggestions for an opening prayer, two such prayers are provided.

OPENING PRAYER
(Suggestion 1)

Watch thou, dear Lord,
with those who wake, or watch, or weep tonight,
and give thine angels charge over those who sleep.
Tend thy sick ones, Lord Christ.
Rest thy weary ones.
Bless thy dying ones.
Soothe thy suffering ones.
Pity thine afflicted ones.
Shield thy joyous ones.
And all, for thy love's sake.

Amen.

Augustine, fourth century monk and author
(http://www.worldprayers.org)

OPENING PRAYER
(Suggestion 2)

The Lord is faithful in all his words,
and gracious in all his deeds.
The Lord upholds all who are falling,
and raises up all who are bowed down.

The eyes of all look to you,
and you give them their food in due season.
You open your hand,
satisfying the desire of every living thing.

The Lord is just in all his ways,
and kind in all his doings.
My mouth will speak the praise of the Lord,
and all flesh will bless his holy name
forever and ever.

Psalm 145:13-17, 21 (NRSV)

ACTIVITY 2:
FINDING MEANING THROUGH SUFFERING

Time: About fifteen to twenty minutes

Objective: To explore how physical ailment can spur one's own spiritual growth and increase one's empathy for those who suffer

- Please read the following:

> Experiencing an illness, disability, or physical suffering often requires us to call on our spiritual resources. This process may result in one finding meaning, and hence spiritual growth, through one's suffering. It also may create a sense of empathy for others who suffer in a like manner. The following activities speak to these two matters.

Experiencing Physical Suffering

The following quote is from a person who deals with cystic fibrosis (CF)—a hereditary life-threatening chronic respiratory disease.

- Read the quote aloud. (This quote is by L. Wood and is quoted in Canda, 2001, p. 113.)

> "So how does God turn a horrible disease into something that could shape a life—my life, your life—for His purpose, His glory and our good. . . . How we respond to suffering makes all the difference. Most would say that pain and suffering should be avoided at all costs, but I believe that by handling it correctly, it can be a teacher to lead us into being people of better character. We need to ask ourselves, 'Do we want to let this make us bitter or better?'. . . . I can honestly say that I am thankful to God because He has used it [CF] to shape me into the person I am . . . becoming."

Follow-Up Activity: Learning from Illness

- Distribute Handout 2.1.
- Ask everyone to take a few moments and write one or two significant physical illnesses or injuries they have experienced.
- Then ask everyone to take a few minutes to reflect on how these experiences required them to call on their faith.
- Ask everyone to briefly answer the Questions to Consider on this handout.
- These questions can be used to help guide their self-reflection and as prompts to begin a discussion.

HANDOUT 2.1. Learning from illness.

Think of one or two physical illnesses or injuries you have experienced; then consider the following questions.

Questions to Consider

1. What type of questions/answers relating to your faith did your experience cause you to seek?

2. How did your faith, religious participation, or spirituality help you respond to this ailment?

3. In what manner, if any, did you gain a sense of empathy with others who similarly suffer?

4. How, if it all, did your experience make you better rather than bitter?

ACTIVITY 3:
PRAYERFUL PHYSICAL ACTIVITY

Time: About fifteen to twenty minutes

Objective: To explore ways that physical activity serves as an aid to prayer

Exercise and Prayerful Contemplation

Sometimes a physical endeavor (such as walking or gardening) can serve to promote one's communion with God. This may be especially true if surrounded by God's works in nature. In addition, some have found that labyrinth walks accomplish the same dynamic.

A labyrinth, as opposed to a maze, only allows one choice of direction. Labyrinth walks became popular in the Middle Ages as a way to symbolize going on a pilgrimage. The labyrinth set in the stone floor of the Chartres Cathedral in France is the most famous and still exists today. In recent times, people take part in labyrinth walks to benefit from the calming effect the circular paths seem to induce. Walking them helps people focus their attention on God while engaging in quiet prayer.

The following activity combines walking with prayer.

- Read the following directions for this activity. (You may find it helpful to prepare a few suggestions for routes to walk in advance.)

Choose a route that you believe will take approximately seven to eight minutes to walk. This should be a route that requires no decision making concerning direction. While walking this route, engage either in prayer or reflection on some spiritual matter, or just be open to the presence of God in the world around you. By practicing this, you can learn to take a prayerful approach to all your physical activities, such as exercise, washing dishes, or yard work.

- Upon return, you may use the following questions to prompt discussion.

Questions to Consider

1. How, if at all, was the experience of praying/contemplating in this manner different from how you normally do it?

2. Have there been times when you have experienced a deep communion with God while engaged in a particular physical endeavor? If so, how can you increase this kind of prayerful physical activity?

ACTIVITY 4:
THE CONNECTION BETWEEN RELIGIOUS
PARTICIPATION AND PHYSICAL HEALTH

Time: About fifteen to twenty minutes

Objective: To explore the ways that religious participation promotes physical health and well-being

Part 1: Examining the Scientific Evidence

- Read the following paragraph aloud:

> In the past twenty years, scientific interest in the spiritual and religious dimensions of health has grown significantly. Prestigious scholarly journals such as the *Journal of the American Medical Association* and the *American Journal of Public Health* have published articles examining this connection. Empirical evidence found in hundreds of studies documents the strength of this relationship. Over half of U.S. medical schools now address spiritual topics in their curricula. In addition, millions of individuals in the United States have turned to what is often deemed alternative or complementary medicine to discover new ways of integrating health concerns and spiritual insights. Despite ongoing debates, it is undeniable that the scientific community is identifying many religion and health connections.

- As time permits, display Overhead 2.1 (Scientific Connections Between Faith and Physical Health) and read its information to participants. Then ask the corresponding questions for discussion.

OVERHEAD 2.1.
Scientific connections between faith and physical health.

In a 1998 study, 440 patients at a suburban family medicine clinic were randomly surveyed. Participants were asked about their level of healthfulness and their personal connection with God or a Higher Power. Results demonstrated that persons with a high or moderately high relationship with God were much more likely to experience better health. As the research team noted, "Differences in health were greatest between patients having a low level of spirituality and those with either moderate or high levels" (McBride, Arthur, Brooks, & Pilkington, 1998, pp. 122-126).

Question: *In your opinion, how can a relationship with God promote overall well-being?*

In a 1998 study, researchers examined nearly 4,000 people aged sixty-five and older. They discovered that people who both attended religious services at least once a week and prayed or studied the Bible at least daily had consistently lower blood pressure than those who did so less frequently or not at all. Furthermore, regular participants in religious activities were 40 percent less likely to have diastolic hypertension, a leading contributor to heart attacks and strokes (Koenig et al., 1998, pp. 189-213).

Question: *In your opinion, why might attending religious services or being involved in a faith community lead to health benefits such as lower blood pressure?*

In a 1999 study, a sample of more than 21,000 American adults tracked over a nine-year period was examined. Researchers found that attending religious services more than once per week raises the possibility of greater longevity. Dr. Robert Hummer and colleagues at the Population Research Center at the University of Texas at Austin reported that, "For the overall population, the life expectancy gap between those who attend more than once a week and those who never attend is over seven years" (Hummer, Rogers, Nam, & Ellison, 1999, pp. 1-13).

Question: *In your opinion, why would involvement in a spiritual community increase one's longevity?*

Part 2: Religious Contributors to Physical Health

- Read the following aloud:

Religion and spirituality frequently prompt the faithful to adopt behaviors and habits that improve their physical well-being. Studies on how faith contributes to one's overall physical health fall into four main categories. First, faith can exert a powerful influence in helping individuals avoid risk behaviors, for example, overindulgence in drinking, smoking, or sexual promiscuity. Second, faith can serve to influence one in adopting positive behaviors, for example, a healthy diet and exercise. Third, faith aids in the development of a strong social support network of family, friends, and religious community members. While social support is extremely beneficial to one's mental health, it can also influence one's physical health through the group support one receives through belonging to a group such as Weight Watchers or through a commitment to exercise together. Finally, one may receive health benefits through the positive effects of prayer.

- Distribute Handout 2.2.
- Ask participants to take a few minutes to reflect on and record how their religious participation has improved their physical health.
- Questions follow that can then be used to prompt a discussion.

HANDOUT 2.2. Inventory of religiously based positive health habits.

Risk behaviors avoided:

Healthy behaviors adopted:

Social support networks:

Experience of healing prayer by self and others:

Questions to Consider for Handout 2.2

1. How does your relationship with God promote physical well-being in your life?

2. How has your involvement in your religious community impacted the four contributors to physical health described earlier (i.e., avoidance of risk behaviors, adoption of positive behaviors, development of a strong social support network, and prayer)?

SUMMING UP

Objective: To summarize what was learned in today's lesson

- You may use the following as guides for summarizing today's lesson:

> Today we explored some possible connections between faith, religious practice, and physical health.

- Choose whichever apply.

Finding Meaning Through Suffering

> We discovered that, when coping with a physical ailment, we may call on our spiritual resources. Such an act can support the healing and recovery processes as well as deepen our faith and appreciation of the spirituality within us. We saw this in. . . . [Use specific examples from the lesson.] It can also serve to increase our level of empathy for others who suffer. We saw this in. . . . [Use specific examples from the lesson.]

Physical Activity As an Aid to Prayer

> We experimented and reflected on how physical activity may aid prayer. This in turn led to considering how a simple physical activity can be instilled with spirituality. Some examples we found were. . . . [Use specific examples from the lesson.]

Religious Influence on Contributors to Physical Health

> We looked at how one's religious participation affects one's physical health through the adoption of positive health habits. Some particular examples of this were. . . . [Use specific examples from the lesson.]

- Conclude with the following:

Conclusion

> Our explorations today were a brief introduction to the connection between faith and physical health. For those of you who have an interest in further exploration, feel free to examine the lesson(s) we were unable to complete today. In addition, supplemental activities are provided that can help you think about and explore these issues more deeply.

- Note: Those who wish to explore any lessons independently will need copies of the directions from the Leader's Guide.

SUPPLEMENTAL ACTIVITY A:
PRAYER AND HEALING

Time: Fifteen minutes

Objective: To explore the use of imagery as a way to bring out the connection between prayer and healing

- Ask participants to silently read the following testimonial (Handout 2.3) concerning Reverend Matthew H. Gates. It describes the role of prayer for him during his experience preparing for open-heart surgery.
- Use Questions to Consider for Handout 2.3 as prompts for discussion.

HANDOUT 2.3. Prayer and healing.

The following is a testimonial concerning Reverend Matthew H. Gates. It describes the role of prayer for him during his experience preparing for open-heart surgery.

Reverend Gates arrived at Boston Memorial Hospital to undergo open-heart surgery. His doctor briefly visited him two nights before the operation. The doctor stated that he would talk with him again the morning of the operation. The operation was scheduled for the afternoon.

Reverend Gates has long believed that complete health requires a harmony between body and soul. Thus, in the many hours of waiting leading up to the operation, he got to work preparing himself spiritually. He viewed this as his area in which to contribute to the success of the surgery.

When the doctor arrived the morning of the surgery, he asked Reverend Gates how he felt. Reverend Gates stated that he was completely at ease and free of anxiety. He described his current state as a "holy calm" that had settled on him. He began explaining that the past two days he had been doing spiritual imaging exercises to help prepare himself for the surgery. He pointed to the four IV bags hanging over his head and explained how he used them to fashion a metaphor. Just as the IV bags, drop by drop, were preparing his body for the surgery, Reverend Gates imagined two spiritual IV bags ministering to him. One of the spiritual IV bags came from without, and one came from within.

The spiritual IV from without he described as, "the prayers and thoughts of my family, my friends, and my former colleagues in ministry. They were being gathered at the feet of God, and drop by drop by drop they were feeding into my psyche and my soul, bringing new strength and confidence." He noticed the doctor listening with interest.

The spiritual IV from within he described as, "all the verses, bits of scripture or hymns, and the lines from great prayers of the church that had been running through my mind. When I couldn't remember words, I would hum the hymn tune, and the message would get through. Drop by drop by drop, this IV began shaping and strengthening my outlook, my faith, my hope as I focused on the goodness, the love, the caring, and the constancy of God. Together, they made me grateful for all that had been and hopeful for all that was to be" (p. 82).

Inspired by Reverend Gates' revelation, the doctor picked up Reverend Gates' Bible and suggested making a covenant between them: "I offer my best surgical skills, you bring your sense of holy calm, and we'll both trust God to make this a successful surgery" (p. 82). Reverend Gates reflected that this was the holiest moment of bonding between doctor and patient he had ever experienced.

Source: Adapted from Wagner, 1993, pp. 81-83.

Questions to Consider for Handout 2.3

1. In your own life, how have you used imagery with prayers of healing or wellness?

2. How have you been affected by reflecting on scripture, hymns, and/or prayers supporting your physical health?

3. Have you experienced a similar *holy calm* during a time of illness? If so, how did it come about?

4. How can these ideas lead you to increase your use of prayer to support your health and healing?

SUPPLEMENTAL ACTIVITY B:
CEREMONY AND HEALING

Time: Twenty minutes

Objective: To explore the role of ceremony as a way to nurture spirituality in daily routines

- Preparation Note: Provisions must be made beforehand to have a small pitcher of water, clean towels, and some type of basin/bowl.
- Read the following:

> Ceremony can serve as a complement to prayer. Ceremonial washing is associated with physical and spiritual cleansing. This activity will give each member an opportunity to both bestow and receive this anointment.

- Begin by stating that everyone will have the opportunity to participate if they so choose, but that you will first begin by demonstrating the ceremony to be used today. Because it is assumed that the people attending today's session are in relatively good health, the ceremony and prayer will be for continued wellness (but can be adapted to support healing if necessary). To conduct the ceremony, you must secure a volunteer who wishes to be anointed.

Ceremony: Washing of the Hands

Step 1: Take a moment to discuss the symbol at work in this ceremony—water as representing the cleansing power of prayer.
Step 2: Next, pour some of the water over the participant's hands. As you are doing this, invoke a simple prayer for God's healing grace to continue to foster health and well-being.
Step 3: Continue by repeating the ceremony. The person who was just anointed now should become the anointer, and a new anointee should come forth.

Thus, this process repeats itself until all who desire it have both bestowed and received an anointment.

- Upon completion of the activity, use the following questions as prompts for discussion.

Questions to Consider

1. What ways, if any, was this experience different from prayer alone?

2. How might one instill a health-related activity of daily life (such as exercise) with spirituality?

SUPPLEMENTAL ACTIVITY C:
MEANING THROUGH SUFFERING

Time: Fifteen minutes

Objective: To explore how fasting and/or abstinence can increase one's empathy for those who suffer

Fasting and Abstinence

- Please read the following:

When fasting or observing abstinence, one embraces hunger for a short duration. Consequently, the experience of fasting may spark insights concerning such suffering. Moderate fasting may also result in benefits to both one's physical and spiritual health. There are different types of fasting. Fasting may include skipping one meal, eating only one meal during the day, eating no food but drinking juice, or eating no food and drinking only water.

- Distribute Handout 2.4 offered below for participants to read individually.
- After this is complete, use Questions to Consider to prompt discussion.

HANDOUT 2.4. Christian tradition and fasting.

Fasting has a long history within the Christian tradition as an aid to prayer. The Bible has numerous references in this regard, beginning with Moses (Exodus 34:28-29). Beyond merely abstaining from food, it is also a time to express repentance and embrace an abstinence from sins. It is seen as a way to surrender to God and thereby achieve a deeper communion with Him (see Matthew 4:4 NIV: Jesus answered, "It is written: 'Man does not live on bread alone, but on every word that comes from the mouth of God'"). Fasting is therefore seen as an opportunity for a spiritual "cleansing"—one that mirrors the cleansing of the body.

In addition, taking inspiration from Isaiah 58:7, NIV ("Is it not to share your food with the hungry . . . ?") by fasting, some people gain a deeper empathy for those who hunger. Consequently, they adopt the practice of donating the money they would have spent on a meal(s) to charities that serve the hungry.

*Physical Health Benefits of Fasting**

When you fast, you give a break in the workload of your digestive organs (stomach, intestines, pancreas, gallbladder, and liver). This downtime is especially beneficial to your liver. Your liver is the prime organ in charge of producing substances that serve to break down unhealthy chemicals circulating in your body. This process is referred to as *detoxification*. Thus, extra time is spent in cleansing toxins from your blood and lymph nodes.

In addition, as the production of new toxins (from the breakdown of food) is temporarily halted, the toxins stored in areas such as your colon, kidneys, bladder, lungs, and skin are released back into your blood to be cleansed. In fact, every cell in your body is allowed an opportunity to "catch up" on its work of eliminating waste that results from consuming nutrients. This is particularly helpful in countering problems that result from overeating or from a sedentary lifestyle.

This entire process is what lies behind the statement that fasting allows the body to "cleanse" itself. Furthermore, some believe that this cleansing process when observed on a regular basis not only may serve to aid in disease prevention but also may serve to slightly slow down one's aging processes.

Note: It is *strongly* recommended that you consult your doctor if you want to fast and plan to do so for more than two days, are pregnant, take daily medications, or suffer from one of the following conditions: anemia, diabetes, ulcers, cancer, blood disease, hypoglycemia, seizures, or problems with your heart, thyroid, kidney, or colon.

---

*Adapted from http://www.healthy.net/scr/Article.asp?ID=1996 (retrieved February 22, 2006).

Questions to Consider for Handout 2.4

1. What experience, if any, have you had with fasting/abstinence? How did it benefit you physically?

2. What are your views regarding how fasting can serve as an aid to prayer?

3. Do you feel that suffering from hunger, from a fast or otherwise, has deepened your empathy for those who continually go hungry? Share some reflections you may have had regarding this.

Session 3

Faith and Mental Health

St. Patrick's Church, New Orleans, Louisiana.

Those of steadfast mind you keep in peace—in peace because they trust in you. Trust in the Lord forever, for in the Lord God you have an everlasting rock.

Isaiah 26:3-4 (NRSV)

If any of you is lacking in wisdom, ask God, who gives to all generously and ungrudgingly, and it will be given you.

James 1:5 (NRSV)

You must make every effort to support your faith with goodness, and goodness with knowledge, and knowledge with self-control, and self-control with endurance, and endurance with godliness, and godliness with mutual affection, and mutual affection with love.

2 Peter 1:5-7 (NRSV)

Health Through Faith and Community
Published by The Haworth Press, Inc., 2006. All rights reserved.
doi:10.1300/5595_04

Time: Fifty minutes plus optional fifty minutes for supplemental activities

Materials:

- Leader's Guide
- Pens/pencils/scratch paper
- Overhead projector
- Overhead transparencies and handouts

Intention: To introduce participants to issues concerning the relationship between faith and mental health

Objectives: During this session, participants will

1. Learn about recent scientific evidence concerning the relationship between faith and mental health.
2. Explore various ways that the Bible addresses issues of wisdom, understanding, suffering, and hope.
3. Consider the religious supports helpful for recovery from distress and mental illness.
4. Be offered a chance to reflect on prayer as a vehicle for the overcoming of psychological distress and for the promotion of well-being.

Learning Activities

Setting Intention Through Welcome and Prayer (five minutes)

- Introduce yourself briefly (if necessary). Briefly share your interest in the present topic.
- Welcome participants and encourage them to ask questions or contribute to discussions throughout the meetings.
- Summarize the accomplishments from previous sessions. The following paragraphs may be utilized for this purpose. Adapt them according to the activities completed.

The first two sessions of this study guide have encouraged us to view health in relation to Christian faith and have allowed us to explore the connection between our faith and our physical health.

In Session 1, we began to explore our own understandings of health and spirituality. In Session 2, we recognized ways in which spirituality and physical health currently complement each other in our life. We explored new ways in which spirituality can be drawn upon to enrich our physical health. We also examined how the interaction between physical health and faith can offer a bridge toward empathizing with the health of one's community and those who suffer within it.

- Ask for a moment of quiet and either offer a short prayer or invite a participant to offer one that sets an intention for participants to be open to learning and supporting each other. (See Activity 1 for suggested prayerful reflections.)

Introducing Activities Related to Session 3 (five minutes)

- Please read the following:

Today's session will focus on how our faith can support peace of mind as well as help us face adversities. Faith allows us to better cope with stress, frustration, hopelessness, and other aspects of our mental health.

- If you have chosen ahead of time one or two of the following activities for this session, read the appropriate descriptions in the following boxes (feel free to choose one of the supplemental activities as a main activity if you feel it best suits your group's needs).
- If you wish to allow time to let the group choose the activities for today's session, read the activity descriptions to introduce possible topics for exploration in today's lesson. Allow the group to choose one or two of the activities for completion during today's session.

Activity 2—Introducing the Scientific Research (about fifteen to twenty minutes)
In this activity, we briefly examine what scientific research has to say about the connection between religious involvement and mental health.

Activity 3—Wisdom and the Book of Proverbs (about fifteen to twenty minutes)
In this activity, we turn to the Book of Proverbs to discover insights into the connection between faith and mental health.

Activity 4—The Symbolism of the Cross and Recovery from Addictions and Mental Illness (about fifteen to twenty minutes)
In this activity, we explore how the cross can be embraced as a symbol for dealing with addictions and mental illness.

Group Activities and Discussion (about thirty-five to forty minutes)

- Begin the first chosen activity, and conduct a group discussion. Prompts for group discussion are included in the activities under Questions to Consider.
- If time allows, begin the second chosen activity.

Concluding Reflections (five minutes)

- Ask participants for any concluding comments.
- Provide a summary and wrap-up of the meeting (see Summing Up).
- Thank participants and inquire into the group's interest in the optional supplemental activities (to work on either independently or at the next meeting).

Supplemental, In-Group, or Take-Home Activities (fifty minutes)

Remaining unexplored themes can be used as supplemental activities, allowing extended time for discussion or reflection.

You and/or participants can use Supplemental Activities A through C for resources within an extended meeting time or for independent learning. In Supplemental Activity A we turn to the story of Job as a source of inspiration when dealing with adversities in life. Supplemental Activity B furthers this examination of dealing with adversity by encouraging reflection and discussion of the Serenity Prayer and its use for such occasions. Supplemental Activity C suggests ways that congregations can develop support systems to assist those suffering from severe mental illness.

ACTIVITY 1:
SETTING INTENTION
THROUGH WELCOME AND PRAYER

Time: Five minutes

Objective: To welcome participants and to set an intention for learning

- Introduce yourself briefly, including your interest in the present topic.
- Welcome participants, and encourage them to ask questions or contribute to discussions throughout the meetings.
- Ask for a moment of quiet and either offer a short prayer or invite a participant to offer one that sets an intention for participants to be open to learning and supporting each other. If you are interested in suggestions for an opening prayer, two such prayers are provided.

OPENING PRAYER
(Suggestion 1)

Rejoice in the Lord always;
Again I will say, Rejoice.
Let your gentleness be known to everyone.
The Lord is near.

Do not worry about anything,
but in everything by prayer and supplication with thanksgiving
let your requests be made known to God.

And the peace of God,
which surpasses all understanding,
will guard your hearts and your minds in Christ Jesus.

Philippians 4:4-7 (NRSV)

OPENING PRAYER
(Suggestion 2)

Lord, make me an instrument of Thy peace;
where there is hatred, let me sow love;
where there is injury, pardon;
where there is doubt, faith;
where there is despair, hope;
where there is darkness, light;
and where there is sadness, joy.

O Divine Master,
grant that I may not so much seek to be consoled as to console;
to be understood, as to understand;
to be loved, as to love;
for it is in giving that we receive,
it is in pardoning that we are pardoned,
and it is in dying that we are born to eternal life.

Amen.

Francis of Assisi, thirteenth-century monk
(http://www.worldprayers.org)

ACTIVITY 2:
THE CONNECTION BETWEEN RELIGIOUS
PARTICIPATION AND MENTAL HEALTH:
EXAMINING THE SCIENTIFIC EVIDENCE

Time: About fifteen to twenty minutes

Objective: To examine how scientific findings support a connection among religious participation, faith, and mental health and relate these findings to your own personal experiences

- Please read the following while displaying Overhead 3.1:

> In a 2001 book that examined a century of research on the topic of religion and health, authors Harold Koenig, Michael McCullough, and David Larson found 100 studies that analyzed the relationship between religion and mental well-being. Of those studies, 79 percent reported at least one positive relationship between religious involvement and greater happiness, life satisfaction, and morale. The research demonstrated that religious participation is commonly linked with results such as alleviating depression; lessening the likelihood of suicide; decreasing the severity of psychological distress; combating alcohol and drug abuse; reducing juvenile delinquency; promoting marital stability; and fostering optimism and hope (Koenig, McCullough, & Larson, 2001, pp. 101-213). The studies cited in this activity represent only a tiny amount of available evidence that supports a spirituality-mental health connection. By examining and discussing these results, however, one is offered an introductory glimpse into the nature of this vital relationship.

- Next display Overhead 3.2 (Scientific Connections Between Faith and Mental Health) and read its information to participants.
- Ask the corresponding questions for discussion.

OVERHEAD 3.1. The connection between religious participation and mental health.

- **2001 book examined 100 studies that analyzed relationship between religiousness and mental well-being.**
- **79 percent reported at least one positive correlation between religious involvement and greater happiness, satisfaction, etc.**
- **Religious commitment and participation have been shown to be associated with**

  —**Less likelihood of depression**
  —**Less likelihood of suicide**
  —**Decreased severity of psychological distress**
  —**Less likelihood of alcohol or illicit drug use**
  —**Reduced juvenile delinquency**
  —**Increased marital satisfaction**
  —**Increased sense of optimism and hope**

Source: Koenig, McCullough, & Larson, 2001 (pp. 101-213).

OVERHEAD 3.2.
Scientific connections between faith and mental health.

A 1991 study conducted in New Haven, Connecticut, randomly sampled 720 adults to examine how religious association and attendance affected levels of psychological distress. Researchers concluded that persons who attend religious services regularly reported lower levels of psychological distress than infrequent attenders and nonattenders. As stated by a co-author of the study, "Our findings indicate that religion may be a potent coping strategy that facilitates adjustment to the stress of life" (Williams, Larson, Buckler, Heckmann, & Pyle, 1991, pp. 1257-1262).

Question: *In your experience, how might prayer or attending a religious service lower levels of psychological distress?*

In a study of the effects of depression on hospitalized patients published in 1998, researchers at Duke University found that the more religious a patient was, the more quickly he or she recovered from depression. The researchers examined eighty-seven patients aged sixty or older who were diagnosed with a depressive disorder. They found that as the level of religious intensity increased, so did the speed of recovery from illness. David B. Larson, MD, of the National Institute for Healthcare Research, observed, "This study indicates that we physicians should encourage our patients to draw on their religious beliefs to work through such a crisis" (Koenig, George, & Peterson, 1998, pp. 536-542).

Question: *In your experience, how has your faith been particularly useful for cultivating positive mental health?*

A study conducted at the University of New Mexico found that the risk for alcohol dependency is 60 percent higher among drinkers with no religious affiliation. According to the author of the study, Dr. William R. Miller, "The abuse of alcohol, which interestingly came to be called 'spirits,' is in some manner incompatible with spirituality" (Miller, 1998, pp. 979-990).

Question: *In your experience, how can religious values, faith, and spirituality help prevent abuse of alcohol and harmful drugs?*

ACTIVITY 3:
WISDOM AND THE BOOK OF PROVERBS

Time: About fifteen to twenty minutes

Objective: To draw insights from the Book of Proverbs that can aid one's mental well-being

- Please read the following:

> In this activity, we will each be examining one or two proverbs to reflect on what wisdom they hold for us today concerning mental health. If possible, try and recall specific anecdotes that reflect your proverb.

- Allow a few minutes for participants to silently read the introductory paragraph and accompanying proverbs in Handout 3.1.
- Allow participants to take turns choosing a proverb or two to reflect on.
- Allow a few minutes for participants to reflect on their chosen proverb.
- After participants have contemplated their individual quotations, either divide the class into small groups (perhaps five to a group) or reconvene as one large group.
- Ask each participant to share thoughts about and explanations of his or her proverb. Allow others to briefly comment, but allow enough time so that each participant who wants to share a proverb can do so.

HANDOUT 3.1. Wisdom and the Book of Proverbs.

A proverb is a short pithy saying in widespread use that expresses a basic truth or practical precept. The Book of Proverbs in the Old Testament is an example of wisdom literature. Proverbs, Job, and Ecclesiastes offer advice concerning practical ethical behavior while sometimes addressing ultimate religious questions such as the problem of evil. *Proverb* translates from the Hebrew term *mashal,* which means a "statement of truth" or "standard of appropriate behavior." These insights can be applied on the personal, community, and social levels and thus offer the opportunity for wide-ranging interpretation and reflection.

Through maintaining a continuous focus on issues of mindfulness, knowledge, and understanding, the Book of Proverbs serves as an ancient example of the relationship between spirituality and mental health. Following are some examples.

1. "The beginning of wisdom is this; Get wisdom, and whatever else you get, get insight." (Proverbs 4:7)
2. "If you are wise, you are wise for yourself; if you scoff, you alone will bear it." (Proverbs 9:12)
3. "When pride comes, then comes disgrace; but wisdom is with the humble." (Proverbs 11:2)
4. "Whoever loves discipline loves knowledge, but those who hate to be rebuked are stupid." (Proverbs 12:1)
5. "By insolence the heedless make strife, but wisdom is with those who take advice." (Proverbs 13:10)
6. "The wise are cautious and turn away from evil, but the fool throws off restraint and is careless." (Proverbs 14:16)
7. "A tranquil mind gives life to the flesh but passion makes the bones rot." (Proverbs 14:30)
8. "The mind of one who has understanding seeks knowledge, but the mouths of fools feed on folly." (Proverbs 15:14)
9. "Folly is a joy to one who has no sense, but a person of understanding walks straight ahead." (Proverbs 15:21)
10. "The mind of the righteous ponders how to answer, but the mouth of the wicked pours out evil." (Proverbs 15:28)
11. "The human mind plans his way, but the Lord directs the steps." (Proverbs 16:9)
12. "The mind of the wise makes their speech judicious, and adds persuasiveness to their lips." (Proverbs 16:23)
13. "One who spares words is knowledgeable; one who is cool in spirit has understanding." (Proverbs 17:27)
14. "A fool takes no pleasure in understanding, but only in expressing personal opinion." (Proverbs 18:2)
15. "Those with good sense are slow to anger, and it is their glory to overlook an offense." (Proverbs 19:11)
16. "Listen to advice and accept instruction, that you may gain wisdom for the future." (Proverbs 19:20)
17. "The purposes in the human mind are like deep water, but the intelligent will draw them out." (Proverbs 20:5)

18. "By wisdom a house is built, and by understanding it is established; by knowledge the rooms are filled with all precious and pleasant riches." (Proverbs 24:3-4)
19. "Know that wisdom is such to your soul; if you find it, you will find a future, and your hope will not be cut off." (Proverbs 24:14)
20. "Do not answer fools according to their folly, or you will be a fool yourself." (Proverbs 26:4)
21. "Four things on earth are small, yet they are exceedingly wise; the ants are a people without strength, yet they provide their food in the summer; the badgers are a people without power, yet they make their homes in the rocks; the locusts have no king, yet all of them march in rank; the lizard can be grasped by the hand, yet is found in kings' palaces." (Proverbs 30:24-28)

Note: All biblical quotations are taken from the New Revised Standard Version of the Bible.

ACTIVITY 4:
THE SYMBOLISM OF THE CROSS
AND RECOVERY FROM ADDICTIONS AND MENTAL ILLNESS

Time: About fifteen to twenty minutes

Objective: To explore how the symbol of the cross has been used in your experiences to help ease mental strain or overcome mental and behavioral problems

- Read the following while displaying Overhead 3.3 (The Symbolism of the Cross and Recovery from Addictions and Mental Illness).

> In his 1985 work, *Let Go, Let God,* John Keller, a Christian pastor and leader in the treatment of drug addiction, offered the symbol of the Christian cross as a useful spiritual symbol to help individuals recover from addiction. We can consider how this also can be relevant to recovery from other mental illnesses or behavioral problems. Keller discussed both the up-and-down ("vertical") movement of spirituality (one's relationship to the divine) and the side-to-side ("horizontal") movement of spirituality (one's relationship to other human beings) as integral for hope and healing. Many suffering from alcoholism and other addictions find religion and spirituality to be vital for their recovery and well-being. Yet, religious support is often overlooked by treatment professionals. Only a small percentage of doctors and therapists address the spiritual needs of patients. Even church communities may sometimes choose to stress the differences between those with substance abuse or mental illness and those without, rather than noting the ways that everyone shares a common human condition (Keller, 1985).

- Use Questions to Consider for Overhead 3.3 as prompts for discussion. Feel free to use your discretion and choose those issues that you think will inspire the most interest from your class. Be sure to emphasize the holistic nature of recovery from substance abuse and prompt participants to think about how such holism might be reflected within the symbolism of the cross.

Please note: Serious mental illness or substance abuse issues of participants should not be dealt with directly in this session. If such issues arise, you should privately advise the person to contact a mental health professional. If you suspect that the person may be a danger to self (e.g., risk of suicide) or others, discuss the situation with your clergyperson as soon as possible to consider referral to a mental health professional. See Supplemental Activity C for more on this topic.

OVERHEAD 3.3. The symbolism of the cross and recovery from addictions and mental illness.

- Cross as useful tool for understanding spiritual support systems
- Vertical length of cross—human-divine relationship
- Horizontal width of cross—human-human relationships
- Necessary to stress both parts for treatment of and recovery from addiction and mental illness
- Churches and congregations must stress the common human condition rather than differences between those with addictions or mental illness and others if hope and healing are to be encouraged.

Source: Keller, 1985.

Questions to Consider for Overhead 3.3

1. In your experience, how can the vertical dimension of spirituality (one's relationship with God) assist in overcoming addictions, mental illness, stress, behavioral problems, and/or frustration over life's struggles and promote a positive mental outlook?

2. In your experience, how can the horizontal dimension of spirituality (one's fellowship with other congregants and use of medical, psychological, and social services or individuals experiencing similar afflictions) assist in overcoming addictions, mental illness, stress, behavioral problems, and/or frustration over life's struggles and promote a positive mental outlook?

3. What does our congregation currently do to help those struggling with addiction, stress, or mental illness? What further actions might be taken to increase a sense of fellowship with and lend support to such individuals?

SUMMING UP

Objective: To summarize what was learned in today's lesson

- You may use the following as guides for summarizing today's lesson:

> Today we explored some possible connections between faith, religious practice, and mental health.

- Choose whichever apply.

Examining the Scientific Evidence

> We looked at three studies, all of which reported a positive relationship between one's level of religious participation and mental health. Examining our own situation, we testified about how this is so in our own life. . . . [Use specific examples from the lesson.]

Wisdom and the Book of Proverbs

> We each read one or two proverbs and reflected on what wisdom these proverbs hold for us today regarding our mental health. Some of the insights that we came up with are. . . . [Use specific examples from the lesson.]

The Symbolism of the Cross and Recovery from Mental Illness

> In this activity, we explored how the cross serves to symbolize both vertical and horizontal aspects of faith, the vertical representing our relationship to God and the horizontal representing our relationship to others. Within our discussion, we related how we might draw on this symbolism as an aid for our mental well-being. We saw this. . . . [Use specific examples from the lesson.]

- Conclude with the following:

Conclusion

> Our explorations today were a brief introduction to the connection between faith and mental health. For those who have an interest in further exploration, feel free to examine the activities we were unable to complete today. In addition, supplemental activities are provided that can help you think about and explore these issues more deeply.

- Note: Those who wish to explore any lessons independently will need copies of the directions from the Leader's Guide.

SUPPLEMENTAL ACTIVITY A:
SUFFERING, FAITH, AND HOPE:
THE EXAMPLE OF JOB

Time: About fifteen to twenty minutes

Objective: To draw inspiration from the example of Job by exploring how one's faith helps one through hardships

- Have volunteers read each of the following paragraphs from Handout 3.2.
- Prompt participants to think, while these are being read, about the ways that Job used faith to deal with physical, mental, spiritual, and social dis-ease and adversity. (If done individually, read the paragraphs and then reflect on the Questions to Consider for Handout 3.2.)
- If done as a group, use Questions to Consider to prompt discussion.

HANDOUT 3.2. About the Book of Job.

The Book of Job is a masterpiece of religious thought that dramatizes the plight of a human being whose tragic sufferings inspire him to question the ethical nature of a God who permits evil and unmerited pain. The prologue features two scenes in God's heavenly court in which He and the Adversary (Satan) agree to test Job's loyalty. Job is presented as a thoroughly upright and godly man who in no way deserves the evils inflicted on him. As God declares, "There is no one like him on the earth" (Job 1:8). Appearing before the heavenly throne, the Adversary suggests that Job will not remain loyal if deprived of family, property, and reputation. God accepts this challenge and withdraws the protection that has previously shielded Job from misfortune.

After this deal has been struck, bandits sweep away Job's flocks and herds; the "fire of God" consumes his sheep and shepherds; and a fierce wind demolishes the house where Job's children are feasting, killing them all. Stripped of everything he holds dear, Job still blesses God's name (1:13-2:21). Satan next persuades God to infect his faithful worshipper with a painful and disfiguring disease, and, although God initially protests this persecution, it eventually comes upon Job.

In Chapter 3 and following, Job prays to have the process of creation reversed, claiming that it is better not to be born than to endure undeserved pain. The hero is then joined by three friends who insist that his misery must be the result of some unknown sin. Job denies their assertions and begins to question why God would allow bad things to happen to good people.

Beginning in Chapter 9, Job challenges God to appear before him as a human being so that his afflictions may be explained. As he states, "I shall say to God, 'Do not condemn me; let me know why you contend against me. Does it seem good to you to oppress, to despise the work of your own hands and favor the schemes of the wicked?'" (10:2-3). When God does appear, however, it is not in a human form. Speaking from a whirlwind, He emphasizes the enormous distance between divine and human understandings of God. Refusing to answer any of humanity's questions about the ethical principles by which He rules the universe, God calls for humility in the face of His ultimate power and understanding. Finally, Job reaffirms his faith. As he asserts in Chapter 42, "I know that you can do all things, and that no purpose of yours can be thwarted. 'Who is this that hides counsel without knowledge?' Therefore I have uttered what I did not understand, things too wonderful for me, which I did not know" (42:2-3).

Job's concept of God and of the divine-human relationship is radically altered by these revelations. Contrary to his friends' suggestions, Job learns that the God-centered world is not based on a justice of retaliation: human misery is not simply punishment for wrongdoing. In the book's epilogue, Job becomes wealthier than before and begets more sons and daughters to replace those who have been killed. However, this restoration and blessing do not fully resolve the perplexing issue of evil and undeserved suffering that continues to pervade human experience.

Note: All biblical quotes from the New Revised Standard Edition of the Bible.

Questions to Consider for Handout 3.2

1. Can you recall instances in your own life when you've faced hardships and felt like Job? If so, what helped you get through them?

2. How have you come to accept or question the explanation that God works in mysterious ways unfathomable to human creation? Share your insights.

3. Can you think of other stories that help you make sense of human suffering?

SUPPLEMENTAL ACTIVITY B:
MENTAL HEALTH AND THE SERENITY PRAYER

Time: About fifteen to twenty minutes

Objective: To explore the role of prayer in helping to facilitate mental well-being

- Please read the following paragraphs while displaying Overhead 3.4:

> There is no shortage of conjecture as to who wrote the Serenity Prayer. Records from Alcoholics Anonymous (AA) show that Dr. Reinhold Niebuhr, of the Union Theological Seminary in New York City, composed it in 1932 as the ending to a longer prayer. In 1934, Dr. Howard Robbins, Niebuhr's friend and neighbor, requested permission to use that portion in a book of prayers he was putting together at the time. It was published that year in Dr. Robbins' book of prayers. In 1939, it came to the attention of an early AA member who liked it so much that he brought it to Bill Wilson, the cofounder of AA. He and his staff read the prayer and felt that it particularly suited the needs of AA. Copies of the prayer were printed and passed around, and the simple statement became an important part of the AA movement.
>
> Another popular idea is that Reinhold Niebuhr actually credited Friedrich Oetinger, an eighteenth-century theologian, for writing the Serenity Prayer. This account suggests that in 1947 Niebuhr read the prayer in an obituary notice in the *New York Tribune* and was so taken by it that he shared it with Bill Wilson. Although we have no certainty about its origin, we know that it was Niebuhr who translated the prayer into English and brought it to prominence in the United States.
>
> In recent years, discussions of the relationship between prayer and health have flourished. The media, the medical community, and churches of all varieties have sought to understand the nature of this connection and the ways that prayer might be employed to improve individual and social well-being. The Serenity Prayer is the most well-known example of a prayer meant to improve mental health. Employed by many in the Recovery Movement and elsewhere, Niebuhr's words have helped millions to improve their sense of well-being and to overcome a variety of psychological stresses.

- Use Questions to Consider for Overhead 3.4 to prompt discussion.

**OVERHEAD 3.4.
Mental health
and the Serenity Prayer.**

- **Dr. Reinhold Niebuhr may have written the Serenity Prayer in 1932.**
- **It came to the attention of an Alcoholics Anonymous member in 1939.**
- **It was brought to Bill Wilson, cofounder of Alcoholics Anonymous.**
- **The prayer was adopted as part of the movement.**
- **Other theories claim that Niebuhr himself shared the prayer with Wilson.**
- **Regardless of its origin, the Serenity Prayer is the most well-known example of a prayer meant to facilitate positive mental health**

THE SERENITY PRAYER

**God, give us grace to accept with Serenity,
The things that cannot be changed,
Courage to change the things
Which should be changed,
And the wisdom to distinguish
The one from the other.**

**Living one day at a time,
Enjoying one moment at a time;
Accepting hardship as a pathway to peace,
Taking, as Jesus did,
This sinful world as it is,
Not as I would have it,
Trusting that You will make all things right,
If I surrender to Your Will,
So that I may be reasonably happy in this life,
And supremely happy with You forever in the next.**

Amen

Source: www.worldprayers.org. For additional information on AA and The Serenity Prayer history, see http://aahistory.com/ prayer.html.

Questions to Consider for Overhead 3.4

1. In your opinion, what changeable and unchangeable things might Niebuhr be alluding to? Provide an example from your own experience if possible.

2. What might Niebuhr mean when he states that "hardship" can be a "pathway to peace"? Can you think of a personal experience that speaks to this point?

3. How might the Serenity Prayer be applied to dealing with your own experience of distress or life challenges to promote your mental health?

SUPPLEMENTAL ACTIVITY C:
CONGREGATIONAL SUPPORTS FOR COPING
WITH SEVERE MENTAL ILLNESS

Time: About fifteen to twenty minutes

- Read the following paragraphs to participants as an introduction to this activity:

> Pathways to Promise is an interfaith technical assistance and resource center that offers liturgical and educational materials, program models, and networking information to promote a caring ministry toward people with serious mental illness and their families.

- Distribute Handout 3.3 and allow participants time to read it.
- Use Questions to Consider for Handout 3.3 as prompts for discussion.

HANDOUT 3.3. Responses to people with mental illness.

Pathways to Promise has observed various responses of faith communities to members who have a severe mental illness, such as schizophrenia. Some responses are very supportive and helpful while others increase the distress of the person with mental illness and his or her family members. These responses include:

- *The person is fully welcomed in worship and congregational activities.* The person's distinctive spiritual style and behaviors, even if unusual, are included and appreciated. Accommodations are made for the person's experience of a mental disability. Cooperation and collaboration between clergy, congregation members, the person with mental illness, and mental health professionals is well established.
- *The person feels unwelcome and stigmatized in the congregation.* The person is regarded as strange. Congregation members convey feelings of awkwardness, distance, or discrimination. The congregation members do not collaborate with the person, family members, and mental health professionals. In this case, the family members might attend services and leave their loved one who has a mental illness at home.
- *The person with a mental illness and family members feel so unwelcome that they all cease attending services entirely.*

Source: Summarized from Shifrin, 1999, *Pathways to understanding: A manual on ministry and mental illness,* pp. 1-30.

Questions to Consider for Handout 3.3

1. Have you ever had experience with someone in your congregation who has a severe mental illness? If so, how did you or others respond to this situation?

2. In the handout, there is a range of three responses to a person with severe mental illness. In the examples you gave in response to question 1, where did people's responses fall in this range?

3. How might the congregation have demonstrated more compassion, knowledge, acceptance, and love?

4. How might the Bible or the doctrines of your religion be guides for assisting someone with a severe mental illness?

5. How can you help clergy and lay staff in your congregation to expand their knowledge about cooperative relationships with local mental health consumer support groups, mental health centers, psychiatrists, social workers, crisis counselors, and other mental health professionals?

Session 4

Faith and Spiritual Health

Cross at Podbrdo Hill, Medjugorje Pilgrimage Site, Bosnia and Herzegovina.

Pursue love and strive for the spiritual gifts.

1 Corinthians 14:1 (NRSV)

Like newborn infants, long for the pure, spiritual milk, so that by it you may grow into salvation.

1 Peter 2:2 (NRSV)

For those who live according to the flesh set their minds on the things of the flesh, but those who live according to the Spirit set their minds on the things of the Spirit.

Romans 8:5 (NRSV)

The Spirit helps us in our weakness. We do not know what we ought to pray for, but the Spirit himself intercedes for us with groans that words cannot express. And he who

Health Through Faith and Community
Published by The Haworth Press, Inc., 2006. All rights reserved.
doi:10.1300/5595_05

searches our hearts knows the mind of the Spirit, because the Spirit intercedes for the saints in accordance with God's will.

Romans 8:26-27 (NIV)

Then Jesus was led up by the Spirit into the wilderness to be tempted of the devil. He fasted forty days and forty nights, and afterwards he was famished. The tempter came and said to him, "If you are the Son of God, command these stones to become loaves of bread." But he answered, "It is written, one does not live by bread alone, but by every word that comes from the mouth of God."

Matthew 4:1-4 (NRSV)

Time: Fifty minutes plus optional fifty minutes for supplemental activities

Materials:

- Leader's Guide
- Pens/pencils/scratch paper
- Overhead projector
- Overhead transparencies and handouts

Purpose: To explore principles, stages, and activities of faith development that lead to a sense of holistic health and well-being

Objectives: During this session, participants will

1. Learn about a model of faith development.
2. Be exposed to a brief history and background of Christian prayer.
3. Assess their current personal spiritual practices.
4. Identify and commit to a regular spiritual practice that facilitates well-being and the embodiment of Christian values in daily life.

Learning Activities

Setting Intention Through Welcome and Prayer (five minutes)

- Introduce yourself briefly (if necessary). Briefly share your interest in the present topic.
- Welcome participants and encourage them to ask questions or contribute to discussions throughout the meetings.
- Summarize the accomplishments from previous sessions. The following paragraphs may be utilized for this purpose. Adapt them according to the activities completed.

    The first three sessions of this study guide have encouraged us to view health in relation to Christian faith; allowed us to explore the connection between our faith and our physical health; and introduced us to the relationship between faith and mental health.

    In Session 1, we began to explore our own understandings of health and spirituality. In Session 2, we explored themes of suffering and of health promotion. Last time, in Session 3, we learned about recent scientific studies describing the relationship between spirituality and mental health. We discovered various ways that the Bible speaks of wisdom, understanding, suffering, and hope, and we reflected upon the power of the cross as a symbol for easing mental stress.

- Ask for a moment of quiet and either offer a short prayer or invite a participant to offer one that sets an intention for participants to be open to learning and supporting each other. (See Activity 1 for suggested prayerful reflections.)

Introducing Themes Related to Session 4 (five minutes)

- Please read the following:

Today's session will concentrate on the topics of faith and prayer, two important pillars to our spiritual health.

- If you have chosen ahead of time one or two of the following activities for this session, read the appropriate descriptions (feel free to chose one of the supplemental activities as a main activity if you feel it best suites your group's needs).
- If you wish to allow time to let the group choose the activities for today's session, read the following activity descriptions to introduce possible topics for exploration in today's lesson. Allow the group to choose one or two of the activities for completion during today's session.

Activity 2—Stages of Faith Development (about fifteen to twenty minutes)
   In this activity, we explore various stages of faith development and their expression in our lives.

Activity 3—Deepening Our Experience of Prayer (about fifteen to twenty minutes)
   In this activity, we look at various reasons why people pray and reflect on how we use prayer in our own lives.

Activity 4—Spirituality Survey (about fifteen to twenty minutes)
   In this activity, we reflect on how our spirituality and faith find expression in our lives and support us in both good times and bad. We then take time for each of us to share some of our reflections/stories with the group.

Group Activities and Discussion (about thirty-five to forty minutes)

- Begin the first chosen activity and conduct a group discussion. Prompts for group discussion are included in the activities in Questions to Consider.
- If time allows, begin the second chosen activity.

Concluding Reflections (five minutes)

- Ask participants for any concluding comments.
- Provide a summary and wrap-up of the meeting (see Summing Up).
- Thank participants and inquire into the group's interest in the optional supplemental activities (to work on either independently or at next meeting).

Supplemental, In-Group, or Take-Home Activities (fifty minutes)

   Unexplored themes can be used as supplemental activities, allowing extended time for discussion or reflection.
   You and/or participants can use Supplemental Activities A and B for resources within an extended meeting time or for independent learning. Both offer an extended look at prayer. Supplemental Activity A draws on the work of Thomas à Kempis to encourage reflection on prayerful attitudes. Supplemental Activity B further explores our investigations into various methods of praying by offering information on Centering Prayer.

ACTIVITY 1:
SETTING INTENTION THROUGH WELCOME AND PRAYER

Time: Five minutes

Objective: To welcome participants and to set an intention for learning

- Introduce yourself briefly, including your interest in the present topic.
- Welcome participants and encourage them to ask questions or contribute to discussions throughout the meetings.
- Ask for a moment of quiet and either offer a short prayer or invite a participant to offer one that sets an intention for participants to be open to learning and supporting each other. If you are interested in suggestions for an opening prayer, two such prayers are provided.

OPENING PRAYER
(Suggestion 1)

**Image of God
born of God's breath
vessel of divine Love
after his likeness
dwelling of God
capacity for the infinite
eternally known
chosen of God
home of the Infinite Majesty
abiding in the Son
called from eternity
life in the Lord
temple of the Holy Spirit
branch of Christ
receptacle of the Most High
wellspring of Living Water
heir of the kingdom
the glory of God
abode of the Trinity.
God sings this litany
eternally in his Word.
This is who you are.**

**"A Litany of the Person," anonymous Trappist monk
(http://www.worldprayers.org)**

OPENING PRAYER
(Suggestion 2)

Father, I abandon myself into your hands;
do with me what you will.
Whatever you may do, I thank you:
I am ready for all, I accept all.
Let only your will be done in me,
and in all Your creatures—
I wish no more than this, O Lord.

Into your hands I commend my soul;
I offer it to you with all the love of my heart,
for I love you Lord,
and so need to give myself,
to surrender myself into your hands,
without reserve,
and with boundless confidence,

For you are my Father.

Charles de Foucauld, late nineteenth- and early
twentieth-century mystic and martyr
(http://www.worldprayers.org)

ACTIVITY 2:
STAGES OF FAITH DEVELOPMENT

Time: About fifteen to twenty minutes

Objective: To explore stages of faith development as they relate to our own lives

- Please read the following:

James Fowler (1991, 2000) and his colleagues have applied the writings of psychologists and philosophers such as Erik Erikson and Lawrence Kohlberg to the Christian faith. Fowler has proposed a model for stages of faith development. These stages are layered in that one retains the insights of the previous stage during personal growth. For example, primal faith of infancy remains at the core of religious experience. This model is presented as a learning tool, as well as to provide inspiration to continue on our spiritual journeys. The ages indicated for each stage are not absolute. They simply reflect periods of life in which these stages typically emerge. According to Fowler, the universalizing faith perspective is not commonly achieved, but we all have the potential. What follows are Fowler's seven stages of faith development.

Let us examine this model as a way to begin a discussion of our understandings of how our lives of faith are developing.

- Display Overhead 4.1 and ask volunteers to read each of the stage definitions.
- Use Questions to Consider for Overhead 4.1 as prompts for discussion.

OVERHEAD 4.1.
Stages of faith development.

1. **Primal faith (infancy):** This stage arises from relations, care, and nurturing love as first experienced by the infant. Caregivers constitute our first experience of omnipotent power and wisdom.

2. **Intuitive-projective faith (early childhood):** This stage begins with the child's awakening to the world of symbols and stories of a religious tradition. These symbols enrich the child's sense of meaning and provide guidance and reassurance.

3. **Mythic-literal faith (middle childhood):** In this stage, faith involves a reliance on the stories, rules, and implicit values of the caregiver's culture and religion. Knowing the stories of "our people" becomes important for defining self and others.

4. **Synthetic-conventional faith (adolescence):** This stage may emerge as a strongly felt worldview and sense of self. In this stage one draws together (synthesizes) stories, values, and beliefs into a worldview. One composes a "story of my stories"—a sense of the meaning and purpose for one's life.

5. **Individuative-reflective faith (young adulthood):** In this stage, a person examines and makes critical choices about his or her identity and faith, for example, whether to retain, modify, or change one's commitment to the faith tradition in which a person was raised.

6. **Conjunctive faith (early midlife):** This stage involves combining personal and societal experiences that may contain contradictions. Conjunctive faith brings a sense of truth that is multifaceted and complex; it includes a genuine openness to the truths of traditions and communities other than one's own.

7. **Universalizing faith (midlife to late life): Letting go of divisive attitudes and behaviors at this stage, the person easily transcends self-oriented thinking and establishes a sense of deep communion with God. Universalizing faith is recognizable in any culture or spiritual tradition. While upholding the importance of one's own particular faith commitment, the person has a sense of compassionate and respectful acceptance of the worth and unity of all people.**

Questions to Consider for Overhead 4.1

1. Which stage of faith, if any, best characterizes how you would describe yourself? Explain why and give an example. If Fowler's model does not fit your viewpoint, please explain why.

2. Tell a story that illustrates some important event that was a turning point in your developing life of faith. How did it impact your ideals for health and community well-being?

3. Describe your ideal for your future faith development. You do not need to use Fowler's terms. Indicate two or three qualities that you hope to achieve. Then consider how you can encourage your continued faith development.

ACTIVITY 3:
REASONS FOR PRAYER

Time: About fifteen to twenty minutes

Objective: To explore various approaches to prayer

- Display Overhead 4.2 (A Brief History of Christian Prayer) and read through it with participants. Feel free to add to this information with the more detailed history given in the following text.

A Brief History of Christian Prayer

The origins of Christian prayer can be found in the prayers of Judaism.

- The Psalms constituted the core of early Jewish prayer, beginning in the fifth century BC.
- Psalms were most likely the regular prayers of Jesus.
- Monks in the Roman Catholic and Eastern Orthodox traditions still recite psalms as a large part of their prayer regimen.
- Jesus made two crucial contributions of widely used Christian prayers: The Lord's Prayer and his words at the Last Supper.
- The version of the Lord's Prayer found in the Gospel of Matthew (6:9-13) is the piece of prayer most widely used by Christians.
- "Giving thanks" *(eucharistia)* in the memory of Jesus, as was done at the Last Supper, has remained the central public prayer of the Christian community.
- The Eucharist is not only a reenactment of Christ's final meal but is also a signal of faith in the future until he comes again.
- By the fourth century AD, the simple early Eucharist had become a stately, highly ceremonial occasion for prayer.

In addition to important public prayers, Christianity has also developed a tradition of largely unstructured private prayer.

- Jesus was remembered as someone who often prayed alone.
- Eastern Christianity developed a body of mystical writings for use during personal prayer beginning in the sixth century AD.
- This style of private prayer began to influence Western Christianity widely during the twelfth century AD.
- Important figures for the mystical tradition in the West include Anselm, Bernard, Richard Rolle, Meister Eckhart, Teresa of Avila, and Thomas à Kempis.
- All these writers emphasized union of the soul with God through the practice of prayer.
- Reformers in the Protestant tradition were primarily antimystical. Thus, the master texts of the art of prayer in the sixteenth and seventeenth centuries were almost all written by Roman Catholics, such as Ignatius Loyola and Francis de Sales.
- In the modern day, such mystical works are read by the faithful across the Christian spectrum. (Hastings, 2000; Rahner, 1975).

*   *   *

- Distribute Handout 4.1, which includes sections on how Jesus prayed and reasons for prayer. Ask participants to briefly review this material.
- Use Questions to Consider for Handout 4.1 as prompts for discussion.

OVERHEAD 4.2. A brief history of Christian prayer.

- **The origins of Christian prayer can be found in the prayers of Judaism.**
- **The Psalms constituted the core of early Jewish prayer, beginning in the fifth century BC.**
- **Psalms were most likely the regular prayers of Jesus.**
- **Jesus made two personal contributions to widely used forms of Christian prayer: The Lord's Prayer and his words at the Last Supper.**
- **The version of the Lord's Prayer found in the Gospel of Matthew (6:9-13) is the prayer most widely used by Christians.**
- **"Giving thanks" *(eucharistia)* in the memory of Jesus, as was done at the Last Supper, has remained the central public prayer of the Christian community.**
- **In addition to important public prayers, Christianity has also developed a tradition of personal private prayer.**
- **Eastern Christianity developed a body of spiritual writings for use during personal prayer beginning in the sixth century AD.**
- **This style of private prayer began to influence Western Christianity widely during the twelfth century AD.**
- **Important figures for this tradition in the West include Anselm, Bernard, Richard Rolle, Meister Eckhart, Teresa of Avila, and Thomas a` Kempis.**
- **All these writers emphasized communion of the soul with God through practice of prayer.**
- **The major texts of the art of private prayer in the sixteenth and seventeenth centuries were almost all written by Roman Catholics, such as Ignatius Loyola and Francis de Sales. In the modern day, however, such works are read by the faithful across the Christian spectrum.**

Source: Hastings, 2000; Rahner, 1975.

HANDOUT 4.1. Prayer.

How Jesus Prayed

The Gospels contain many references to Jesus praying, including the following:

- *Matthew 14:23:* Jesus went up on the mountain by himself to pray.
- *Matthew 26:36-44:* Jesus went with three disciples, left them behind, and went further to pray alone. This is the well-known passage in which his disciples fall asleep at Gethsemane prior to Jesus' arrest and execution and is mentioned in all three synoptic gospels.
- *Mark 1:35:* Jesus went to a solitary place to pray.
- *Luke 3:21:* This passage describes how Jesus was baptized and was in prayer when the Holy Spirit descended.
- *Luke 5:16:* Jesus is described as often going to lonely places to pray by himself.
- *Luke 6:12:* Jesus withdrew to a mountainside to pray. Verse 13 implies that he was alone at the time.
- *Luke 9:18:* Jesus was praying alone, with his disciples in the vicinity.
- *Luke 22:41-43:* Jesus withdrew from his disciples "about a stone's throw" to pray by himself.
- *John 16:1-18:1:* Jesus first talked to his disciples, then he prayed, then he went with his disciples across the Kidron Valley.

Some Reasons Christian People May Have for Prayer

- The purpose of all Christian prayer is communion with God.
- Prayer is a harmonization of the inward and outward human being.
- During prayer, God promises to hear and answer according to God's will.
- Prayer seeks God's will in faith.
- Prayer has the capacity to change things in God's created universe.
- Prayer offers petitions for guidance and deliverance.
- Prayer shows love and respect toward God.
- Prayer may seek God's grace for issues of personal health, family well-being, community well-being, and world peace.

Questions to Consider for Handout 4.1

1. Which statements offered within the Some Reasons for Prayer list match best with your own reasons for prayer? Provide an example.

2. What additions, if any, would you make to this list?

3. Why do you think Jesus so often prayed alone?

4. Can you identify any ways you could enhance your own practice of personal prayer to nurture your continuing spiritual development?

ACTIVITY 4:
SPIRITUALITY SURVEY

Time: About fifteen to twenty minutes

Objective: To reflect on the current level of spiritual activity in our lives

- Allow approximately ten minutes for participants to record their answers to the Spirituality Survey questions (Handout 4.2).
- Begin a discussion in which you ask people to share their answers to the Spirituality Survey questions.

HANDOUT 4.2. Spirituality survey.

This outline is designed to help each participant to assess his or her own current level and quality of spiritual activity. It is intended to provide the individual and the group with a place of reference for planning future goals regarding spiritual activities and to be a vehicle to share experiences and insights with others.

1. What type of spiritual activities (such as Bible reading, prayer, journal writing, listening to inspirational music) do you perform alone? Together with your family at home? With a group, such as at church? Please describe each of these activities.

2. What are the most significant stories, teachings, or symbols that give you guidance in life?

3. What personal experiences have given you a sense of peace, wisdom, or grace?

4. What spiritual supports have helped you the most in a time of crisis?

5. What spiritual supports have helped you the most in a time of great satisfaction or joy?

6. How can you build on or increase your spiritual activities and experiences to promote your continuing spiritual development?

Source: Adapted from Canda & Furman, 1999.

SUMMING UP

Objective: To summarize what was learned in today's lesson

- You may use the following as guides for summarizing today's lesson:

> Today we explored ways to nurture our spiritual development. Our discussions yielded a number of interesting insights.

- Choose whichever apply.

Stages of Faith Development

> In this activity, we explored various stages of faith development as proposed by Fowler. Our discussion yielded the following insights. . . . [Use specific examples from the lesson.]

Reasons for Prayer

> In this activity, we examined the ways that Jesus prayed, noting that he often prayed alone. We also explored various reasons for prayer, such as showing love and respect toward God, union with God, and as petitions for well-being of ourselves, loved ones, and the world. Some of our conclusions were as follow. . . . [Use specific examples from the lesson.]

Spirituality Survey

> In this activity, we took a few minutes to reflect on how our spirituality finds expression in our lives and how it supports us in both good times and bad. We each had an opportunity to share some of these reflections. . . . [Use specific examples from the lesson.]

- Conclude with the following:

> Our explorations today were a brief introduction to the various aspects of spirituality. For those who have an interest in further exploration, feel free to examine the lesson(s) we were unable to attend to today. In addition, two supplemental activities on prayer are provided.

- Note: Those who wish to explore any lessons independently will need copies of the directions from the Leader's Guide.

SUPPLEMENTAL ACTIVITY A:
CHRISTIAN DEVOTION
AND IMITATION OF CHRIST

Time: Twenty minutes

Objective: To reflect on the devotional nature of prayer

- Read the following paragraph about the life and work of Thomas à Kempis:

> Thomas à Kempis (1380-1471) was a German monk and author who wrote many devotional works. His career culminated with *Imitation of Christ* (1441), a book that celebrated humanity's dependence on God's boundless love. Protestants and Roman Catholics alike joined in giving it praise. The Jesuits gave it an official place among their spiritual "exercises." It greatly affected Thomas More and Ignatius of Loyola. John Wesley and John Newton put it among the works that influenced them at their conversions. Few books have had so extensive a circulation. The number of counted editions exceeds 2,000. For 500 years, this gentle book, filled with the spirit of the love of God, has brought understanding and comfort to millions of readers in over fifty languages (*New Catholic Encyclopedia,* 2003).

- Display Overhead 4.3 and ask for a volunteer to read the passage from Kempis' *Imitation of Christ.*
- Use Questions to Consider for overhead 4.3 as prompts for discussion.

OVERHEAD 4.3. Excerpt from *Imitation of Christ.*

When God gives you spiritual comfort, receive it gratefully, but know it to be a gift from God, not something you deserve. Do not be puffed up with pride, overly glad, or vainly presumptuous, but be all the more humble because of the gift. . . . When you no longer feel the comfort of God's presence, do not despair right away. With humility and patience, wait for the heavenly visit, for God will return a richer comfort to you than you had before. . . . Usually, temptation is a sign of comfort to follow, for heavenly comfort is promised to those who are tried by temptations: "He who overcomes," says the Lord, "shall eat of the tree of life." (Kempis, 1989, pp. 44-45)

Questions to Consider for Overhead 4.3

1. Can you think of instances in your own life where you have faced the challenge of accepting "a gift from God" without being "overly glad" or "vainly presumptuous"?

2. In what ways does your faith assist you to "wait for the heavenly visit" in times of despair?

3. What do you think Kempis means when he writes, "Heavenly comfort is promised to those who have been tried by temptations"? Can you think of personal examples that support this statement?

SUPPLEMENTAL ACTIVITY B:
CENTERING PRAYER

Time: Thirty minutes

Objective: To explore an increasingly popular, although traditional, form of quiet contemplative prayer

- Allow participants a few minutes to silently read the information on Centering Prayer (Handout 4.3).
- Instruct them to find a comfortable place and practice this method once they have finished reading about it. (Normally, you would want to give yourself at least fifteen minutes to pray; however, this time period can be abridged for the purposes of this lesson.)
- Gather the group back together and use Questions to Consider for Handout 4.3 as prompts for discussion.

HANDOUT 4.3. Centering Prayer.

What Is Centering Prayer?

Centering Prayer is a method of quiet prayer that opens oneself to the Holy Spirit. It is an attempt to present the teachings of earlier times in an updated form. It is not meant to replace other kinds of prayer. It simply offers another way to pray. During the time of centering prayer we consent to the Holy Spirit's presence and action within us. At other times our attention moves outward to discover the Holy Spirit's presence everywhere.

Centering Prayer is

- A relationship with the Holy Spirit and a discipline to foster that relationship
- An exercise of faith, hope, and love
- A movement beyond conversation with Christ to communion
- A process that awakens us to the language of the Holy Spirit that is silent

Centering Prayer Basics

1. Choose a short prayer or prayerful word as the symbol of your intention to consent to the Holy Spirit's presence and action within.
2. Sitting comfortably and with eyes closed, silently introduce the prayerful word as the symbol of your consent to the Holy Spirit's presence and action within.
3. When you become aware of thoughts, return ever-so-gently to the prayerful word.
4. At the end of the prayer period, remain in silence with eyes closed for a couple of minutes.

Further Explanation of Centering Prayer Practice

I. "Choose a prayerful word as the symbol of your intention to invite the Holy Spirit's presence and action within."
   1. The prayerful word expresses our intention to be in the Holy Spirit's presence and to yield to the divine action.
   2. The prayerful word should be chosen during a brief period of prayer asking the Holy Spirit to inspire us with one that is especially suitable for us.
      a. Examples: God, Lord, Abba, Jesus, Holy Spirit
      b. Other possibilities: Love, Peace, Faith
   3. Having chosen a prayerful word, we do not change it during the prayer period, for that would be to start thinking again.
   4. A simple inward gaze upon the Holy Spirit may be more suitable for some persons than the prayerful word. In this case, one consents to the Holy Spirit's presence and action by turning inwardly toward it as if gazing upon it. One can simply be aware of the gentle flow of breath as a point of focus. The same guidelines apply to the sacred gaze as to the prayerful word.
II. "Sitting comfortably and with eyes closed, silently introduce the prayerful word as the symbol of your consent to the Holy Spirit's presence and action within."
   1. By "sitting comfortably" is meant relatively comfortably, not so comfortably that we encourage sleep, but sitting comfortably enough to avoid thinking about the discomfort of our bodies during this time of prayer.

2. Whatever sitting position we choose, we keep the back straight if possible.
3. If we fall asleep, we continue the prayer for a few minutes upon awakening if we can spare the time.
4. Praying in this way after a main meal encourages drowsiness. Better to wait an hour at least before Centering Prayer. Praying in this way just before retiring may disturb one's sleep pattern.
5. We close our eyes to let go of what is going on around and within us.
6. We introduce the sacred word inwardly and as gently as laying a feather on a piece of cotton.

III. "When you become aware of thoughts, return ever-so-gently to the sacred word."
1. "Thoughts" is an umbrella term for every perception, including sense perceptions, feelings, images, memories, reflections, and commentaries.
2. Thoughts are a normal part of Centering Prayer.
3. By "returning ever-so-gently to the prayerful word," a minimum of effort is indicated. If not using a prayerful word, simply return to awareness of the breath.
4. During the course of our prayer, the sacred word may become vague or even disappear.

IV. "At the end of the prayer period, remain in silence with eyes closed for a couple of minutes."
1. If this prayer is done in a group, the leader may slowly recite the Lord's Prayer during these two or three minutes, while the others listen.
2. These two or three minutes give our minds time to readjust to the external stimuli and enable us to invite the Holy Spirit into our daily lives.

Some Practical Points

The minimum time for this prayer is fifteen minutes. Two periods are recommended each day, one first thing in the morning and one in the afternoon or early evening.

Points for Further Development

During this prayer, we avoid analyzing our experience and we do not harbor expectations or aim at some specific goal. For example, we do not force ourselves to:

- Repeat the sacred word continuously
- Have no thoughts
- Make the mind a blank
- Feel peaceful or consoled
- Achieve a spiritual experience

Extending the Effects of Centering Prayer into Daily Life

- Practice two periods of Centering Prayer daily.
- Practice Centering Prayer as a prelude to reading from the Bible.
- Study other important books about prayer, meditation, and the spiritual life.
- Join a Centering Prayer support group or follow-up program (if available in your area).
  —It encourages the members of the group to persevere in private and together.
  —It provides an opportunity for further input on a regular basis through tapes, readings, and discussion.
- Attend weekend, weeklong, or even longer prayer retreats.

Source: Adapted from Keating, 1994, 2002.

Questions to Consider for Handout 4.3

1. How is this method of prayer similar to or different from how you usually pray?

2. In what type of circumstances would you see yourself adopting this method of prayer?

Session 5

Faith and the Well-Being
of the Church Community

Sycamore Log Church (near Branson, Missouri).

They devoted themselves to the apostles' teaching and to the fellowship, to the breaking of bread and to prayer. Everyone was filled with awe, and many wonders and miraculous signs were done by the apostles. All the believers were together and had everything in common. Selling their possessions and goods, they gave to anyone as he had need. Every day they continued to meet together in the temple courts. They broke bread in their homes and ate together with glad and sincere hearts, praising God and enjoying the favor of all the people.

Acts 2:42-47 (NIV)

Just as each of us has one body with many members, and these members do not all have the same function, so in Christ we who are many form one body, and each member belongs to all others.

Romans 12:4-5 (NIV)

Health Through Faith and Community
Published by The Haworth Press, Inc., 2006. All rights reserved.
doi:10.1300/5595_06

Jesus called them together and said, "You know that those who are regarded as rulers of the Gentiles lord it over them, and their high officials exercise authority over them. Not so with you. Instead, whoever wants to become great among you must be your servant."

Mark 10:42-43 (NIV)

"I ask not only on behalf of these, but also on behalf of those who will believe in me through their word, that they may all be one. As you, Father, are in me and I am in you, may they also be in us, so that the world may believe that you have sent me. The glory that you have given me I have given them, so that they may be one, so that the world may know that you have sent me and have loved them even as you have loved me."

John 17:20-23 (NRSV)

Time: Fifty minutes plus optional fifty minutes for supplemental activities

Materials:

- Leader's Guide
- Pens/pencils/scratch paper
- Overhead projector
- Overhead transparencies and handouts

Intention: To provide participants with an opportunity to reflect on their communal life as a church and how it fosters individual and community well-being

Objectives: During this session, participants will

1. Increase understanding about interpersonal relationships within church settings.
2. Explore several leadership styles.
3. Examine congregational role structures.
4. Explore various roles one may perform on a church committee or board.
5. Gain understanding about parish nursing and its contributions to the church community's health.

Learning Activities

Setting Intention Through Welcome and Prayer (five minutes)

- Introduce yourself briefly (if necessary). Briefly share your interest in the present topic.
- Welcome participants and encourage them to ask questions or contribute to discussions throughout the meetings.
- Summarize the accomplishments from previous sessions. The following paragraphs may be utilized for this purpose. Adapt them according to the activities completed.

The first four sessions of this study guide have encouraged us to view health in relation to Christian faith; allowed us to explore the connection between our faith and our physical health; introduced us to the relationship between faith and mental health; and helped us reflect on basic principles of the spiritual journey through deepening and expanding prayer.

In Session 1, we began to explore our own understandings of health and spirituality. In Session 2, we explored themes of suffering and of health promotion. In Session 3, we examined how our faith can provide us peace of mind when facing adversity. Last time, in Session 4, we learned about a mode of faith development and the history of Christian prayer, assessed our current spiritual practices, and examined different spiritual exercises that facilitate wellness and embodiment of Christian values.

- Ask for a moment of quiet and either offer a short prayer or invite a participant to offer one that sets an intention for participants to be open to learning and supporting each other. (See Activity 1 for suggested prayerful reflections.)

Introducing Activities Related to Session 5 (five minutes)

- Please read the following:

> Today's activities will focus on the health and vibrancy of our church community.

- If you have chosen ahead of time one or two of the following activities for this session, read the appropriate descriptions (feel free to choose one of the supplemental activities as a main activity if you feel it best suits your group's needs).
- If you wish to allow time to let the group choose the activities for today's session, read the activity descriptions to introduce possible topics for exploration in today's lesson. Allow the group to choose one or two of the activities for completion during today's session.

Activity 2—Interpersonal Relationships Within the Church (about fifteen to twenty minutes)

In this activity, we explore how relationships are nurtured within our church community. It offers an opportunity to recognize the positive relationships that already exist while also challenging us to examine ways to improve engagement in some areas.

Activity 3—Leadership (about fifteen to twenty minutes)

This activity allows us to take a look at various styles of leadership. Then we consider which styles best suit our own personalities as well as the particular situations in our church community.

Activity 4—Congregational Role Structures (about fifteen to twenty minutes)

In this activity, we explore the health of the church community by investigating how individuals' roles within the church respond to change.

Group Activities and Discussion (about thirty-five to forty minutes)

- Begin the first chosen activity and conduct a group discussion. Prompts for group discussion are included in the activities in Questions to Consider.
- If time allows, begin the second chosen activity.

Concluding Reflections (five minutes)

- Ask participants for any concluding comments.
- Provide a summary and wrap-up of the meeting (Summing Up).
- Thank participants and inquire into the group's interest in the optional supplemental activities (either to work on independently or at next meeting).

Supplemental, In-Group, or Take-Home Activities (fifty minutes)

Unexplored activities can be used as supplemental activities, allowing extended time for discussion or reflection.

You and/or participants can use Supplemental Activities A and B for resources within an extended meeting time or for independent learning. Supplemental Activity A explores the role of parish nursing as a way to contribute to the health of the church community. Supplemental Activity B allows us to reflect on our contributions to the church committees and boards on which we serve and how we may more positively embrace such service.

ACTIVITY 1:
SETTING INTENTION
THROUGH WELCOME AND PRAYER

Time: Five minutes

Objective: To welcome participants and to set an intention for learning

- Introduce yourself briefly, including your interest in the present topic.
- Welcome participants and encourage them to ask questions or contribute to discussions throughout the meetings.
- Ask for a moment of quiet and either offer a short prayer or invite a participant to offer one that sets an intention for participants to be open to learning and supporting each other. If you are interested in suggestions for an opening prayer, two such prayers are provided.

OPENING PRAYER
(Suggestion 1)

God of grace, you nurture us with a love deeper than any we know and your will for us is always healing.

God of comfort and strength, revive us when we are weary, console us when we are full of sorrow, and set our feet in the way Christ leads us.

God of peace, fill us with your presence and send us forth, recreated, to act compassionately and in healing ways toward your people everywhere.

We ask this in the name of Jesus Christ by the Holy Spirit.

Amen.

OPENING PRAYER
(Suggestion 2)

I pray that the God of our Lord Jesus Christ, the Father of
   glory,
may give you a spirit of wisdom and revelation as you come to
   know him,
so that, with the eyes of your heart enlightened,
you may know what is the hope to which he has called you,
what are the riches of his glorious inheritance among the
   saints,
and what is the immeasurable greatness of his power for us
   who believe, according to the workings of his great power.

God put this power to work in Christ when he raised him from
   the dead
and seated him at the right hand in the heavenly places,
far above all rule and authority and power and dominion,
and above every name that is named,
not only in this age but also in the age to come.
And he has put all under his feet and has made him the head
   over all things
for the church, which is his body, the fullness of him who fills
   all in all.

                          Ephesians 1:17-23 (NRSV)

ACTIVITY 2:
INTERPERSONAL RELATIONSHIPS WITHIN THE CHURCH

Time: Fifteen to twenty minutes

Objective: To explore how relationships within the community of the congregation can be nurtured

- Please read the following:

> Relationships inside the church reflect the same types of tensions as all human relationships. This occurs because we are all human. Yet interpersonal relationships within the church are blessed in that they have the potential to reflect the love and unity that each member experiences in relationship to God.
>
> In this activity, we seek to recognize in what ways relationships are nurtured in our church. Then we will explore what may be some new ways to nurture relationships.

Recognizing Nurturing Relationships

- Inquire as to who would like to share a quick story of a particularly nurturing relationship that someone has experienced through the church. You may begin this activity by offering to share first.

Exploring New Ways to Nurture

- Direct the participants to take a minute or two to complete the Church Relationship Checklist (Handout 5.1). Emphasize completing it quickly based on one's immediate impressions.
- Once the checklist is complete, use it as a springboard to discuss the Questions to Consider for Handout 5.1. [Note: Encourage participants to connect their answers to question number 1 to the stories related earlier.]
- This activity may stimulate participants to later put some ideas into action. The important point of this activity is to make a commitment with other willing members; specific plans can be elaborated upon at a future date. The final session of this study guide will help people to begin making plans for action, if desired.

The following may serve as source of inspiration for this activity. Lee (1991), a deacon in the United Methodist Church and member of the Asian American Committee on Diaconal Ministry, wrote that laity and clergy need to reach a commitment to shared responsibilities that focus on individual gifts rather than rigid roles and hierarchies. He suggested that clergy and laity

1. come together in harmony between themselves and deity;
2. understand that all people have contributions to make;
3. be wary of rigid role differentiation between laity and clergy;
4. actualize the Kingdom of God through expressing abilities to listen, empathize, risk, heal, and forgive;
5. empower laity; and
6. uphold the concept of fellowship through being—clergy and laity together—the body of Christ.

HANDOUT 5.1. Church relationship checklist.

Circle a number for each of the questions below according to the following scale:

1	2	3	4	5
Never	Rarely	Sometimes	Usually	Always

1. Is your congregation a welcoming congregation to guests and new members?

1   2   3   4   5

2. Is there room for theological differences to be voiced?

1   2   3   4   5

3. Are children effectively engaged?

1   2   3   4   5

4. Are children included in intergenerational activities or in age-specific learning experiences?

1   2   3   4   5

5. Are the needs of older adults addressed?

1   2   3   4   5

6. Are individuals who may be sexual minorities welcome in the congregation?

1   2   3   4   5

7. Are people from racial and ethnic minorities equally welcomed and included in all worship experiences and other activities?

1   2   3   4   5

8. Are individuals of many social classes represented?

1   2   3   4   5

9. Do clergy, lay staff, and congregation members cooperate in a spirit of mutual appreciation and support?

1   2   3   4   5

Total =
Total Possible = 45

Questions to Consider for Handout 5.1

1. For any of the checklist questions that you answered "sometimes," "usually," or "always," share with the group your view on how this occurs.

2. For any of the checklist questions that you answered "never" or "rarely," share with the group why you believe this is so and offer an idea that may improve this area.

3. Share your thoughts on any areas of interest that are not mentioned in the checklist.

4. Write down any of the ideas for improvement that you or the group find particularly important.

ACTIVITY 3:
LEADERSHIP

Time: About fifteen to twenty minutes

Objective: To explore ways in which church members may take on leadership roles

What are the activities of leadership in the church? Communities of faith preserve their values in scripture, the rituals and sacraments, and church tradition. Sometimes congregations are viewed as groups of talented and active contributors. Sometimes they are also seen as passive gatherings of consumers. Different models of leadership bring out different types of responses in the congregation. Various congregations have different areas of strength and different goals. As such, they may seek different types of spiritual leaders as well.

- Please read the following:

> Leaders play an important role in attending to the overall well-being of the church community. Opportunities often arise for individual members to take on the role of a leader for a church activity. This learning activity seeks to examine various styles of leadership and to spur reflection upon how you might contribute as a leader or support a leader.

- Have volunteers take turns reading aloud the paragraphs in Examining Leadership on Overhead 5.1.
- Use Questions to Consider for Overhead 5.1 to prompt discussion.
- *Alternative:* Instead of waiting until all the paragraphs are read, you may stop after each paragraph to accept or elicit examples of each of the leadership styles. (This is question 1 in Questions to Consider.)

OVERHEAD 5.1. Examining leadership.

In taking on the role of a leader, a person adopts a particular style. Jesus modeled various leadership styles at different times in his ministry. Jesus expressed the qualities of prophet, priest, and king, and each demanded a different leadership style. To be most effective, a leadership style should arise based on the context of a situation—for each style has both its strengths and weaknesses. Whitehead and Whitehead (1986) describe four styles of religious leadership that mirror the qualities that Jesus adopted in various situations.

Four Leadership Styles

One style is that of *king*. When the leader wields great decision-making power, a hierarchical system may be put into place to carry out those decisions. This style's strength is that it is effective in promoting the work of a congregation. It is also time efficient, as decisions can be made quickly. This style's weakness is that it does not encourage the diversity of viewpoints and talents that comes when others are involved in directing congregational life.

A second style is that of *father/mother* in a community that thinks of itself as a family. The parental image itself, however, may be perceived positively or negatively depending on one's earliest family experiences. This style's strength is that it promotes a welcoming and comforting tone. Its weakness is that it does not easily offer members the opportunity to contribute as equals.

A third style is that of *servant,* one who models leadership by associating with those who are given little opportunity to voice their concerns. This style's strength is that it offers the greatest opportunity for empowering members, viewing them as talented and active contributors. Its weakness is that decision making is less timely and efficient—everyone's viewpoint is important and must be considered.

A fourth leadership style is that of *steward*. The steward is responsible for important decisions about things that he or she does not own. The steward makes decisions in the owner's absence but with authority (a type of guest authority) given for a certain extent of time. Stewards then carry an inner authority that is expressed in the absence of the owner. The strength of this style is that it offers a trustworthy way in which to delegate authority—allowing multiple projects to be attended to personally. Its weakness is that it relies on the steward to correctly guess the intentions of the owner—and the steward may sometimes guess wrong.

Questions to Consider for Overhead 5.1

1. Discuss a situation in a recent congregational experience that would fit each of the four leadership styles.

2. Which of the four leadership styles do you feel the most comfortable adopting or working with for the benefit of your church community?

3. What is a likely situation in which you could see yourself applying this style or working with a leader who uses this style?

ACTIVITY 4:
CONGREGATIONAL ROLE STRUCTURES

Time: About fifteen to twenty minutes

Objective: To explore to what degree our church-related roles are flexible and adaptable

- Allow time for participants to read Handout 5.2.
- Ask if there are any questions concerning the passage.
- Use Questions to Consider for Handout 5.2 to prompt discussion.

HANDOUT 5.2. Congregational role structures.

Role structures result from predictable patterns (Whitehead & Whitehead, 1986). At first, roles may be openly advertised. However, as tasks are repeated, other members become aware that these individuals are doing a good job, and roles are stabilized into defined role structures. For example, Karen may be comfortable with offering an opening prayer publicly, while Bill may be willing to bake food for the meeting. The same holds true for leadership roles. This system benefits the health of the congregation in that peers recognize individuals' strengths, and the group places people in areas where they build on their current strengths.

If not attended to, however, in time these role structures may become unchangeable and rigid. The roles then begin to be viewed as automatic and exclusive to particular individuals. This may be unfair to both the individual assuming the role (a duty voluntarily embraced becomes expected) and to other members (who may not have the opportunity to share their skills or develop new ones).

Developing a role structure helps meet the goals of the group, but, when roles become fixed and rigid, the congregation loses the flexibility that is necessary as structures change. It is beneficial to the congregation's health for new individuals and old ideas to be challenged. This can serve to validate existing structures as well as promote change. It is also how new leaders emerge and receive training. Structures that encourage change of power at intervals allow for this type of congregational growth and flexibility.

Questions to Consider for Handout 5.2

  1. Have you ever been caught in a rigid role for the church (either willingly or unwillingly)? Share your experience.

  2. If you had the opportunity to take on a new role for the church (or if you have done so recently), what might it be? Share your experience.

  3. In what ways are flexibility and adaptability of roles actively supported in your congregation?

SUMMING UP

Objective: To summarize what was learned in today's session

- You may use the following as guides for summarizing today's session:

> Today we explored various aspects of the well-being of our church community. Our explorations yielded a number of interesting insights.

- Choose whichever apply.

Interpersonal Relationships Within the Church

> We each had an opportunity to share how our church community has fostered a particular special relationship for us. We saw this in. . . . [Use specific examples from the activity.]
> We also looked at ways in which our community can possibly better engage more people. Some ideas that arose were. . . . [Use specific examples from the activity.]

Leadership

> We examined four different styles of religious leadership that were modeled by Jesus: the king, the parent, the servant, and the steward. We found that each of these styles worked well depending on the situation. . . . [Use specific examples from the activity.]
> We also looked inward as to which style best suited us and then imagined a situation where we might contribute as a leader. . . . [Use specific examples from the activity.]

Congregational Role Structures

> We examined how individuals may become "stuck" in a particular role that they assume for the church, such as . . . [Use specific examples from the activity.] We then discussed possible ways to promote turnover in these roles. These included . . . [Use specific examples from the activity.]

- Conclude with the following:

Conclusion

> Our explorations today were a brief introduction to the well-being of our church community. For those of you who have an interest in further exploration, feel free to examine the activity(s) we were unable to attend to today. In addition, supplemental activities are provided that can help you think about and explore these issues more deeply.

- Note: Those who wish to explore any activities independently will need copies of the directions from the Leader's Guide.

SUPPLEMENTAL ACTIVITY A:
SOCIAL HEALTH IN THE CHRISTIAN COMMUNITY:
PARISH NURSING

Time: Twenty-five minutes

Objective: To learn how parish nursing may contribute to the health of the church community

- Please read the following:

> Recently, some programs have been developed that serve as models for congregationally based health and social services provision. Church social work and parish nursing are two of these models. This activity focuses on parish nursing as an example of a successful congregational-level response to maintaining personal health.

The parish nurse program was begun as a result of a partnership between six churches in the Chicago area and Lutheran General Hospital in Park Ridge, Illinois. It was formalized in 1984 by Reverend Granger Westberg. As early as the 1940s, this pastor and teacher began to see the need for preventive medicine within a church context. He opened a clinic within a church consisting of a nurse, a doctor, and a pastor, but it was expensive to operate and hard to sustain. He then approached Lutheran General Hospital, which tested the concept of a parish nurse in preventive health care with six churches: four Protestant and two Roman Catholic. The hospital sponsored the program by paying 75 percent of the half-time salary for each nurse the first year. It steadily decreased the percentage so that by the fourth year each church fully supported the nurse's salary. Because of continuing interest nationwide, a Parish Nurse Resource Center was established in 1986 at Lutheran General Hospital.

In 1995, Lutheran General Hospital was purchased by Advocate Health Care System, and the Parish Nurse Resource center was renamed the International Parish Nurse Resource Center to reflect its expanding scope. In 2001, the center closed but endorsed a standardized curriculum for parish nursing. Content included discussion of the role of the church in health, theology of health, and models of parish nursing. Also taught were functions of the parish nurse as teacher, counselor, referral agent, and integrator of faith and health, as well as practical issues of working in a church context and functioning as part of a ministerial team.

- Read this passage as well:

> Some models of parish nursing primarily use volunteers, while others have paid staff. With the nurse's ability to train volunteers in a church community, care can be extended beyond a traditional health care system. "Through integrating faith and health, the parish nurse draws the power of belief, prayer, ritual and community into the equation of health and healing" (Carson & Koenig, 2002, p. 118).

- Ask participants to now read silently The Parish Nurse's Story (Handout 5.3).
- Afterward, use Questions to Consider for Handout 5.3 to prompt discussion.

HANDOUT 5.3. The parish nurse's story.

Helen's first visit as a parish nurse was a truly memorable experience. It affected her so profoundly that she viewed it as an affirmation from the Lord of her ministry. One Friday afternoon, she received a call from the church secretary. The secretary informed her that one of the parishioners was at the hospital. She was currently in labor; however, the baby was dead. The pastor happened to be out of town, so she requested that Helen visit.

Helen prayed during the entire trip to the hospital, asking God to help her bring comfort to this family. She soon arrived at the hospital and met the young woman, Laura, and her concerned husband and family members. Helen discovered from the husband, Dan, that on Tuesday the baby had stopped moving. An ultrasound examination on Wednesday confirmed their worst fears. Originally, the doctor assumed that labor would start spontaneously; however, it did not. Laura was admitted to the hospital, and labor was induced on Thursday. Helen had arrived late Friday afternoon, and Laura was still in labor.

Helen, being a nurse, was allowed into the delivery room and spoke words of encouragement and support to both Laura and Dan between Laura's contractions. Then, Helen offered to pray with them. It was just a simple prayer, "Lord, we don't know why this is happening. Our hearts are just breaking, but we know that you are in control and that you promise to be with us always. We pray that you will deliver this baby quickly and support Laura and Dan with your love and comfort" (p. 57). Helen left the hospital soon after the prayer. She received a call from Dan the following morning, who told her, "Thank you so much for coming—what a miraculous answer to prayer; about two minutes after you left Laura delivered the baby!" (p. 57).

Helen continued to minister to Laura and Dan over the next weeks. She made regular visits, shared in prayer, and linked them to a number of resources. Although her first experience as a parish nurse is a sad story due to the loss of the baby, when Helen reflected on it, it also brought comfort and inspiration to her. She felt a real sense of how God might call on her as a Christian woman and as a nurse.

Helen views her role as a parish nurse in the following way. Her mission is not to preach or teach to a multitude of persons in a gathering. She holds one hand at a time, hugs one person. She may support one family wresting with the impending death of a parent, or she may sit with one family awaiting a loved one to emerge from surgery. She will never minister to a huge number as a parish nurse, but, for her, parish nursing will always be a ministry of mercy, a ministry of one person at a time.

Source: Adapted from Carson & Koenig, 2002, pp. 56-58.

Questions to Consider for Handout 5.3

1. How does parish nursing promote the health of the community in a way different from a standard nursing role?

2. What activities might be applied from the concept of parish nursing to church or congregational setting?

3. Is there a parish nursing program or church social work program in your congregation? If so, how does it contribute to the health of the church community? If not, voice your opinion on whether it would be desirable to start one.

SUPPLEMENTAL ACTIVITY B:
KOINONIA: BUILDING COMMUNITY
AND FELLOWSHIP

Time: Twenty-five minutes

Objective: To examine how the Bible offers directives for building Christian fellowship

- Please read the following paragraphs to participants:

> Jesus emphasized the importance of Christian communities in Matthew 19:20 when he stated, "For where two or three come together in my name, there am I among them" (NIV). Here, Christ was promoting *koinonia,* the New Testament Greek word for "fellowship," "community," or "communion." This word appears on nearly twenty occasions in the New Testament when authors are providing guidelines for the establishment of Christian communities. Although the term is used most commonly in reference to fellowships among early Christians, today it is increasingly being employed to express ideal congregational relationships and these groups' ability to foster communion with God. In this activity, we will explore biblical passages that offer strategies for building *koinonia* and consider applications for these principles within our own church community.

- Display Overhead 5.2. Read through the quotations and allow participants a few minutes to reflect on their meanings.
- Begin a discussion by using the Questions to Consider for Overhead 5.2 as prompts.

> ## OVERHEAD 5.2. The New Testament on fellowship.

The New Testament instructs Christian communities to

1. "Encourage one another"—1 Thessalonians 5:11
2. "Be hospitable to one another"—1 Peter 4:9
3. "Teach and admonish one another"—Colossians 3:16
4. "Be kind to one another"—Ephesians 4:32
5. "Pray for one another"—James 5:16
6. "Bear one another's burdens"—Galatians 6:2
7. "Welcome those who are weak in faith"—Romans 14:1
8. "Look not to your own interests, but to the interests of others"—Philippians 2:4
9. "Regard each other as better than yourselves"—Philippians 2:3
10. "Become slaves to one another"—Galatians 5:13

Questions to Consider for Overhead 5.2

1. In your opinion, which of these principles is the easiest to enact? Why? Which is the hardest to enact? Why?

2. In your experience, have you witnessed church members who model this notion of *koinonia* especially well in their attempts to "encourage," "be hospitable," "teach," or "be kind" to one another? Share some examples. How have these incidents served to bring to light a sense of *koinonia* in your church community?

3. In your experience, can prayers from those in your congregation or other Christians facilitate health and healing? Please provide specific examples.

4. According to Christian theologian James Evans, *koinonia* refers to the solidarity of the church community in which a common purpose is strong enough to render all other stratification among human beings of only secondary purpose (Evans, 1992). Reviewing quotes six through ten, how has this notion of *koinonia* expressed itself in your church community?

Session 6

Faith and the Well-Being of Society

Mural Detail, Peace Plaza (Rev. Martin Luther King Jr. National Historic Site, Atlanta, Georgia).

For the hurt of my poor people I am hurt, I mourn, and dismay has taken hold of me. Is there no balm in Gilead? Is there no physician there? Why then has the health of my poor people not been restored?

Jeremiah 8:21-22 (NRSV)

The Spirit of the Lord is on me, because he has anointed me to preach good news to the poor. He has sent me to proclaim freedom for the prisoners and recovery of sight for the blind, to release the oppressed, to proclaim the year of the Lord's favor.

Luke 4:18-19 (NIV)

Health Through Faith and Community
Published by The Haworth Press, Inc., 2006. All rights reserved.
doi:10.1300/5595_07

There is no longer Jew or Greek, there is no longer slave or free, there is no longer male and female; for all of you are one in Christ Jesus.

Galatians 3:28 (NRSV)

You are no longer strangers and aliens, but you are citizens with the saints and also members of the household of God, built upon the foundation of the apostles and prophets, with Christ Jesus himself as the cornerstone. In him the whole structure is joined together and grows into a holy temple in the Lord; in whom you are also built together spiritually into a dwelling place for the Lord.

Ephesians 2:19-22 (NRSV)

Time: Fifty minutes plus optional fifty minutes for supplemental activities

Materials:

- Leader's Guide
- Pens/pencils/scratch paper
- Overhead projector
- Overhead transparencies and handouts
- Bibles—at least three, preferably one for each member (Supplemental Activity B)

Intention: To make the connection between Christian faith and community service; to promote the well-being of society

Objectives: During this session participants will

1. Become familiar with the Christian orientation—historical, philosophical, and theological—toward addressing social problems.
2. Identify critical social problems in your community and the larger society that need to be addressed.
3. Identify possible actions to address these problems.

Learning Activities

Setting Intention Through Reflection (five minutes)

- Introduce yourself briefly (if necessary). Briefly share your interest in the present topic.
- Welcome participants and encourage them to ask questions or contribute to discussions throughout the meetings.
- Summarize the accomplishments from previous sessions. The following paragraphs may be utilized for this purpose. Adapt them according to the activities completed.

> The first five sessions of this study guide have encouraged us to view health in relation to Christian faith; allowed us to explore the connection between our faith and our physical health; introduced us to the relationship between faith and mental health; helped us reflect on basic principles of the spiritual journey through deepening and expanding prayer; and encouraged us to reflect on our communal life as a church and how it fosters both individual and congregational well-being.
>
> Last time, in Session 5, we gained an understanding of interpersonal relationships within the church setting, explored church leadership styles, and examined congregational role structures.

- You should take a moment of quiet and either offer a short prayer or invite a participant to offer one that sets an intention for participants to be open to learning and supporting each other. (See Activity 1 for suggested prayerful reflections.)

Introducing Activities Related to Session 6 (five minutes)

- Please read the following:

Today's activities turn our attention to the well-being of the local community and the larger society of which we are a part by investigating how we may address various needs and promote the well-being of society.

- If you have chosen ahead of time one or two of the following activities for this session, read the appropriate descriptions (feel free to choose one of the supplemental activities as a main activity if you feel it best suits your group's needs).
- If you wish to allow time to let the group choose the activities for today's session, read the activity descriptions to introduce possible topics for exploration in today's lesson. Allow the group to choose one or two of the activities for completion during today's session.
- Prior to beginning the chosen activities [e.g., numbers 2, 3, or 4], introduce the topic of social health by completing the preface, titled Social Determinants of Health. The time for this preface is variable, as it is likely that some discussion will arise based on its content. At a minimum it will take five minutes.

Activity 2—Everyday Activities That Lead to Societal Well-Being (about fifteen to twenty minutes)

This activity allows reflection on how each of us already contributes to our society's well-being. From this perspective, society is viewed as being composed of numerous individuals, all potentially contributing to its betterment through their positive involvement in the everyday activities of life.

Activity 3—Faith-Based Community Organizing (about fifteen to twenty minutes)

In this activity, we explore the connections among Christian congregations, community organizing, and service for peace and justice. The focus is on exploring issues relevant to the congregation's local community.

Activity 4—National Organizations and Faith (about fifteen to twenty minutes)

In this activity, we learn about different national organizations that address social issues, such as poverty, racism, and AIDS, from a spiritual perspective. Various ways to volunteer service are explored.

Group Activities and Discussion (about thirty-five to forty minutes)

- Introduce the general topic of social health by completing the preface, Social Determinants of Health.
- Begin the first chosen activity and conduct a group discussion. Prompts for group discussion are included in the activities in Questions to Consider.
- If time allows, begin the second chosen activity.

Concluding Reflections (five minutes)

- Ask participants for any concluding comments.
- Provide a summary and wrap-up of the meeting (see Summing Up).
- Thank participants and inquire into the group's interest in the optional supplemental activities (to work on either independently or at extended meeting).

Supplemental, In-Group, or Take-Home Activities (fifty minutes)

You and/or participants can use Supplemental Activities A and B for resources within an extended meeting time or for independent learning. Supplemental Activity A extends Activity 3 by exploring how our own spiritual health may be stimulated through our volunteer efforts. It offers reflections by an individual who donated time to address a community need and about how this experience contributed to her own spiritual health. In Supplemental Activity B, we turn to biblical verses as a source of inspiration for contributing to one's community.

OVERHEAD 6.1.
Summary of insights about social factors of health.

Thirty years of scientific research on social factors affecting population health suggest the following:

· **Higher income levels are associated with better levels of physical health.**
· **The experience of poverty, even beyond the level of access to basic needs, is a powerful negative influence on health.**
· **Countries with a wide gap between rich and poor, such as the United States, have a *lower* life expectancy than countries with a lesser gap (such as Sweden and Japan).**
· **Some social factors that may have a major negative influence on physical health of community members include the following:**
  —**A greater experience of discrimination, oppression, and low social status.**
  —**Lesser access to health care resources and material conditions that support health (such as quality nutrition, housing, and sanitation).**
  —**Lesser availability of education and social skills preparation for planning and achieving life goals.**
  —**Lesser experience of positive social support networks, such as family, friends, neighborhood, religious groups, and community institutions.**
  —**Lower rates of employment and sense of satisfaction with employment. (Adapted from Tarlov & St. Peter, 2000.)**

Examples of Connections Between Health Risks and Social Situation

According to statistics taken from the National Center for Health Statistics report titled *Health, United States* (2002):

- In 1998, *infant mortality* rates were higher for infants of black, Hawaiian, and Native American mothers (13.8, 10.0, and 9.3 deaths per 1,000 live births) than for infants of other race groups. Infant mortality rates for Hispanic and non-Hispanic white mothers were similar (5.8 and 6.0 per 1,000 life births).

- *Infant mortality* decreases as the mother's level of education increases. This trend is greater for white mothers than for mothers in other racial and ethnic groups. In 1998, mortality for infants of non-Hispanic white mothers with less than a high school education was double that for infants whose mothers who had at least a high school education.

- In 1999, *overall mortality* was one-third higher for black Americans than for white Americans. Preliminary age-adjusted death rates for the black population exceeded those for the white population by 38 percent for stroke, 28 percent for heart disease, 27 percent for cancer, and more than 700 percent for HIV disease.

- The risk for *suicide* is higher for elderly white males than for other groups. In 1999, the preliminary suicide rate for white males aged eighty-five years of age and over was more than three times that for young white males fifteen to twenty-four years of age.

- Between 1992 and 1999, the *occupational injury* death rate increased 15 percent to 4.4 deaths per 100,000 employed workers. The industries with the highest death rates were mining, agriculture, forestry, and fishing (22 to 24 deaths per 100,000). Construction, with a death rate of 14 per 100,000, accounted for the largest number of deaths, 20 percent of all occupational injury deaths. The risk of fatal occupational injury was highest among workers aged sixty-five years and over.

ACTIVITY 1:
SETTING INTENTION
THROUGH WELCOME AND PRAYER

Time: Five minutes

Objective: To welcome participants and to set an intention for learning

- Introduce yourself briefly, including your interest in the present topic.
- Welcome participants and encourage them to ask questions or contribute to discussions throughout the meetings.
- Ask for a moment of quiet and either offer a short prayer or invite a participant to offer one that sets an intention for participants to be open to learning and supporting each other. If you are interested in suggestions for an opening prayer, two such prayers are provided.

OPENING PRAYER
(Suggestion 1)

Blessed be the God and Father of our Lord Jesus Christ,
the Father of mercies and the God of all consolation,
who consoles us in all our affliction,
so that we may be able to console those who are in any
   affliction
with the consolation with which we ourselves are consoled by God.

For just as the sufferings of Christ are abundant for us,
so also our consolation is abundant through Christ.
If we are being afflicted, it is for your consolation and salvation;
if we are being consoled, it is for your consolation,
which you experience when you patiently endure the same
   sufferings
that we are also suffering.

Our hope for you is unshaken;
for we know that as you share in our sufferings,
so also you share in our consolation.

2 Corinthians 1:3-7 (NRSV)

OPENING PRAYER
(Suggestion 2)

You are holy, Lord,
the only God,
and Your deeds are wonderful.
You are strong.
You are great.
You are love.
You are wisdom.
You are humility.
You are endurance.
You are rest.
You are peace.
You are joy and gladness.
You are justice and moderation.
You are all our riches, and You suffice for us.
You are beauty.
You are gentleness.
You are our protector.
You are our guardian and defender.
You are our courage.
You are our haven and our hope.
You are our faith, our great consolation.
You are our eternal life, Great and Wonderful Lord, God
  Almighty,
Merciful Savior.

Francis of Assisi, thirteenth-century monk
(http://www.worldprayers.org)

PREFACE TO SESSION 6 ACTIVITIES 2, 3, AND 4:
SOCIAL DETERMINANTS OF HEALTH

- Display Overhead 6.1 while reading the following paragraph to participants:

> As a preface to today's activities, it is important to consider how factors such as race, ethnicity, sex, age, education, income, and occupation affect both personal and social health in the United States. The following statistics and observations demonstrate that such social factors do indeed have a dramatic influence upon well-being. Think about this information as we progress through our chosen activities, and feel free to integrate it into any of our discussions to follow.

- Read each of the statistics and observations offered on the overhead or solicit volunteers to do the same. Feel free to initiate group discussion if questions or comments arise.

ACTIVITY 2:
EVERYDAY ACTIVITIES THAT LEAD
TO SOCIETAL WELL-BEING

Time: About fifteen to twenty minutes

Objective: To recognize how we already contribute to society's well-being through some of our everyday activities and how we can expand this contribution

- Read the following paragraphs to participants:

> This activity concentrates on how each of us already contributes to our society's well-being through raising children, fulfilling other caretaking roles, devoting oneself to a job, etc. People undertaking these activities in a positive manner help to build a healthy society. Recognizing our personal contributions serves as a basis for appreciating what we already do. We can then consider how we can expand on such duties, obligations, and gifts.
>
> Discussion of questions may bring up participants' ideas about their moral commitments to the good of society. The idea behind these questions is to examine how we do these activities—what makes them a positive contribution. The emphasis should be on the following links: faith—moral code—everyday activities—contributing to society's health.

- Use Questions to Consider as prompts for group discussion.

Note: Be careful that the discussion of these questions does not become a theological and political debate about "right" and "wrong" practices (e.g., specific "right" and "wrong" morals to instill in children). The intent of this exercise is not to assign judgment to actions but rather to simply emphasize taking actions that are of benefit to society.

Questions to Consider

    1. What are some everyday activities of life that you do that serve to contribute to the well-being of society?

    2. In what way do these activities contribute to society's well-being?

    3. In what ways does your faith influence how you do these activities?

    4. How can you improve or expand your contributions to the well-being of society?

ACTIVITY 3:
FAITH-BASED COMMUNITY ORGANIZING

Time: About fifteen to twenty minutes

Objective: To explore how churches organize in order to meet community needs

- Distribute Handout 6.1 and allow participants time to read it.
- Use Questions to Consider for Handout 6.1 as prompts for group discussion.

HANDOUT 6.1. Faith-based community organizing.

Thousands of congregations across the country have engaged their members in collaborative efforts to improve schools, promote economic development, fight crime and violence, and build affordable housing. Jesus carried a message of peace and did not wait passively for the future, but actively organized for change. Jesus was a community organizer, advocating for the poor and the oppressed.

For example, historically, African-American communities have utilized the church as their primary vehicle for spiritual, social, and economic empowerment. The prominence of the church throughout the Civil Rights Movement is well-known. The Reverend Dr. Martin Luther King Jr. helped lead the African-American church into the forefront of the struggle for equal opportunity. The success of this church-based model for social change was unprecedented. The Civil Rights Acts of 1964 and 1965 contained historic changes in voting rights, public accommodations, and fair housing opportunities for African Americans.

In the 1960s and 1970s, some churches built houses, established homeless shelters, and began the process of community revitalization. A rising number of African-American church communities began to take an active role in revitalizing their neighborhoods. For example, since the 1980s, the Reverend Dr. Johnny Ray Youngblood and the East Brooklyn Churches organization have led a massive effort to build more than 2,000 single-family affordable homes through the Nehemiah Project in New York City.

In general, various churches have identified many social issues in their communities as appropriate to address some examples are:

- Affordable housing
- Day care programs
- Computer training centers
- Welfare-to-work programs
- Youth empowerment programs
- After-school programs
- Sponsoring refugees' resettlement
- Food for the hungry

Addressing social problems in the community from a faith perspective is not necessarily always done as a group or solely within the church congregation. Many people of faith have jobs in which they are responsible for attending to social problems or volunteer in various capacities. Some may want to combine these individual activities in the community with a formal community-outreach project of the church. Faith-based initiatives for social service have become widely encouraged. These may involve government and religious cooperative programs, such as refugee resettlement and youth support programs.

Questions to Consider

1. Are there social service activities that you are currently involved in that would benefit from a formal community-outreach project of your church? If not, discuss possible activities. Share your ideas.

2. What social support programs (e.g., day care or a food pantry for homeless) does your church currently organize? If you have been involved in any of these, share how you became involved, that is, what lay behind getting people organized to help.

3. Are there any existing needs in the community that could benefit from a new or expanded organized response by the church?

ACTIVITY 4:
NATIONAL RELIGIOUS ORGANIZATIONS
AND SOCIAL JUSTICE

Time: About fifteen to twenty minutes

Objective: To explore various ways in which one might volunteer time toward improving society's well-being

- Please read the following:

Although our society is strong in many ways, unfortunately there are many ills that continue to plague our society's health. Many of us are moved to address these ills by donating money or goods to worthy causes. The following three examples, however, each suggests a direct way in which individuals can take action (in terms of donating time and effort) in order to contribute toward improving the health of our society. As you reflect on these examples, consider the following statement from the United Methodist Church's Book of Discipline:

> We claim all economic systems to be under the judgment of God no less than other facets of the created order. Therefore, we recognize the responsibility of governments to develop and implement sound fiscal and monetary policies that provide for the economic life of individuals and corporate entities, and that ensure full employment and adequate incomes with a minimum of inflation. We believe private and public enterprises are responsible for the social costs of doing business, such as employment and environment pollution, and that they should be held accountable for these costs. We support measures that would reduce the concentration of wealth in the hands of the few. (*Book of Discipline of The United Methodist Church—2000*, Paragraph 163)

- Display Overheads 6.2 through 6.4. If you desire, feel free to stop after each example and use the Questions to Consider for a brief discussion or reserve the questions until all overheads have been displayed.
- Allow a few minutes of exploration for those interested in "going the extra mile." (See Questions to Consider for Overheads 6.2 throughy 6.4.)

OVERHEAD 6.2. Example 1: Mobilizing to reduce poverty in America.

Action: Writing to Your Congressional Representative and Senators

Action alerts are e-mail telegrams put out by lobbying organizations to alert concerned individuals about upcoming debates on a particular issue. They are used at both the state and federal levels. They allow you to share your views with your legislators in a timely manner.

For example, as recently stated by the National Council of Churches:

> A movement is underway to confront the persistent challenge of poverty in America. It's a joint venture of the National Council of Churches' (NCC) 36 member denominations, dozens of local and regional councils of churches, and national partner organizations such as Children's Defense Fund, Habitat for Humanity, Families USA, and Call to Renewal. (http://www.ncccusa.org)

Ending poverty in the United States is among the NCC's top priorities. Your advocacy with your U.S. Senators and Representatives can help.

Contact information:
National Council of Churches Communication Department
475 Riverside Drive, Suite 880
New York, NY 10115
212-870-2227
Web site: www.ncccusa.org

OVERHEAD 6.3. Example 2: Putting faith into action.

Action: Donating One's Labor

According to Habitat for Humanity International:

> **Habitat's ministry is based on the conviction that to follow the teachings of Jesus Christ we must reflect Christ's love in our own lives by loving and caring for one another. Our love must not be words only—it must be true love, which shows itself in action. Habitat provides an opportunity for people to put their faith and love into action, bringing diverse groups of people together to make affordable housing and better communities a reality for everyone. (http://www.hfhi.org)**

Contact information:
Habitat for Humanity International
121 Habitat St.
Americus, GA 31709-3498
229-924-6935, ext. 2551 or 2552
Web site: http://www.habitat.org/default2.aspx

OVERHEAD 6.4. Example 3: Acting together for respect and justice.

Action: Walking for a Cause

The National Conference for Community and Justice (NCCJ), founded in 1927 as The National Conference for Christians and Jews, is a human relations organization dedicated to fighting bias, bigotry, and racism. The NCCJ promotes understanding and respect among all races, religions, and cultures through advocacy, conflict resolution, and education.

As recently stated by the NCCJ:

> Want to find a way to express your commitment to ending bias, bigotry and racism in your own community? Well, put on your most comfortable walking shoes and join us as we Walk As One!

> While meeting new friends and getting some fresh air and exercise, walkers are able to demonstrate their commitment to a community that is inclusive and just. Through the Walks, individuals, companies, organizations, and community leaders can support NCCJ and promote respect and understanding among all people. Together, we can celebrate our progress in fighting bias, bigotry and racism and take a stand against ongoing issues of intolerance. (http://www.nccj.org)

Contact information:
National Conference for Community and Justice
475 Park Avenue South, 19th Floor
New York, NY 10016
212-545-1300
Web site: www.nccj.org

Questions to Consider for Overheads 6.2 Through 6.4

1. Imagine yourself participating in each of the activities in Overheads 6.2 through 6.4. In what manner would your actions be contributing to society's well-being?

2. In what ways would you draw on your faith in motivating yourself to take such actions as described in each of the three examples?

3. Have you participated in similar activities in the past or other social action activities organized by national groups that involved donating time (as opposed to money or goods)? If so, share these experiences with the group.

4. Going the extra mile: Reflect on your current involvement in contributing to society's health on a national level. Drawing on this recent group discussion, seek a fellow group member who you feel shares your level of interest and commitment in this area. Just as finding oneself an "exercise buddy," discuss with this person how you can motivate each other in pursuing social action activities that appeal to both of you. Make a few initial commitments about finding and sharing information on this mutually agreeable topic.

SUMMING UP

Objective: To summarize what was learned in today's session

- You may use the following as guides for summarizing today's session:

> Today we explored various aspects of the well-being of our society and the connection between individual and social health.

- Choose whichever apply.

Everyday Activities That Lead to Societal Well-Being

> We discussed some important ways we already contribute to our society's well-being through ordinary activities. Examples of this were. . . . [Use specific examples from the activity.]
>
> We also examined how our faith guided us in the performance of these activities. . . . [Use specific examples from the activity.]

Faith-Based Community Organizing

> We explored how the church can act as an organizing institution to tackle various problems in the community. Examples of this were. . . . [Use specific examples from the activity.]
>
> We also looked at some additional needs of the community that could benefit from the organizing power of the church, such as. . . . [Use specific examples from the activity.]

National Organizations and Spirituality

> We examined some major societal needs. We then explored ways to volunteer our service to help address these needs. These were writing your state or federal legislator, volunteering your labor, and walking for a cause. This led us to discuss the role that our faith would play in motivating us to take actions to contribute to society's well-being.

- Conclude with the following:

Conclusion

> Our explorations today were a brief introduction to the connection between faith and social well-being. For those who have an interest in further exploration, feel free to examine the activity(s) we were unable to attend to today. In addition, supplemental activities are provided as well.

- Note: Those who wish to explore any activities independently will need copies of the directions from the Leader's Guide.

SUPPLEMENTAL ACTIVITY A:
SOCIAL HEALTH AND THE CHRISTIAN
COMMUNITY: AN EXAMPLE FROM HABITAT FOR HUMANITY

Time: Twenty-five minutes

Objective: To reflect on how one grows spiritually through contributing to the well-being of society

- Distribute Handout 6.2 and allow participants time to read it, or read it aloud for them.
- Elicit brief responses from the participants regarding the information and their previous knowledge and attitude about this organization.
- Next read the following:
- Use Questions to Consider for Handout 6.2 as prompts for discussion.

HANDOUT 6.2. Social health in the Christian community:
An example from Habitat for Humanity.

In many large cities the number of affordable housing units that are in good condition is small and growing smaller. A recent study by the National Low Income Housing Coalition found that the average cost of renting a two-bedroom apartment and paying for utilities is so high in most states that a person with a minimum-wage job would be unable to find anyplace to live. The social health of a community is clearly influenced when some members struggle to meet basic housing needs.

Habitat for Humanity International (HFHI) was established in 1976 with a goal of eliminating poor housing construction and homelessness. This movement also seeks to make decent shelter a matter of conscience and action. This nonprofit organization is nondenominational and has a Christian foundation. Since its beginning, more than 125,000 houses have been built in eighty countries, including roughly 45,000 houses in the United States.

This program follows what they term the "theology of the hammer." Denominational differences fall into the background as groups that may include individuals of several denominations experience the challenges of channeling faith into action in a common purpose. The program also emphasizes the "economics" of Jesus, which involves sharing resources with those in need while recognizing the ability of those who receive the resources to contribute equally to the community.

Key components of this program include the following three conditions: (1) Future homeowners and volunteers work together under supervision to build a house. (2) The house is sold without profit, and the homeowner is not charged interest on his or her mortgage. (3) Corporations, faith communities, and individuals provide financial support. Local habitat affiliates select partner families based on their ability to repay the no-interest mortgage, their demonstrated need, and their commitment to work with Habitat. Families are chosen without regard to race, ethnicity, or religious affiliation. Payments for housing by partner families (varying from seven to thirty years) are then used to fund the construction of other Habitat houses.

An interesting feature of this program is that affiliate organizations are asked to tithe, giving ten percent of their contributions to fund housing construction in other countries. An ecumenical, international board of directors determines policy and oversees and guides the mission of Habitat for Humanity International. Local affiliates mirror this structure by maintaining their own volunteer boards (Habitat for Humanity International, www.hfhi.org).

Questions to Consider for Handout 6.2

1. Habitat for Humanity is a wonderful example of faith-based volunteerism to benefit the larger community. Think of a time when you have acted to serve someone in need. Share your experience. (What did you do? How was your behavior perceived? Was it understood, valued, accepted?)

2. What meaning did this experience have for you spiritually?

3. How does this encourage you to continue community service or to try a new kind of community service?

SUPPLEMENTAL ACTIVITY B:
BIBLICAL VERSE ACTIVITY
ON COMMUNITY ORGANIZING

Time: Twenty-five minutes

Objective: To seek inspiration for creating positive change in our community through examining the various ways that Jesus created social changes

- Direct participants to break up into three groups. (If you are doing this activity alone as a take-home extension, simply choose one, two, or all three group readings below, as you desire).
- Assign the groups the following biblical verses.
- Ask each group to read and then briefly discuss the various ways that Jesus promoted community service and social justice within these verses. Take no more than ten minutes in these small groups.

The following verses demonstrate various acts of community service and social justice led by Jesus:

Group 1
Christ feeds the hungry   Luke 9:10-17

Group 2
Christ heals the sick   Luke 7:21
Christ rebukes corrupt officials   Luke 19:45-48

Group 3
Christ recognizes dignity in Samaritans   Luke 10:30-37
Christ shows care for dignity in women
   and children   Mark 5:21-43

- Ask participants to gather back into one group in order to share their insights. Questions to Consider can be used as prompts for this discussion.

Questions to Consider

1. What techniques did Christ use to create social change?

2. How can you address these social issues in your own community?

Session 7

Faith and Global Well-Being

Adam and Eve folk art sculptures, Garden of Eden private park, Lucas, Kansas.

He has told you, O mortal, what is good; and what does the Lord require of you but to do justice, and to love kindness, and to walk humbly with your God?

Micah 6:8 (NRSV)

"Because of the oppression of the weak and the groaning of the needy, I will now arise," *says the Lord.*

Psalm 12:5 (NRSV)

The Lord bless you and keep you; the Lord make his face to shine upon you, and be gracious to you, the Lord lift up his countenance upon you, and give you peace.

Numbers 6:24-26 (NRSV)

Health Through Faith and Community
Published by The Haworth Press, Inc., 2006. All rights reserved.
doi:10.1300/5595_08

He raises up the poor from the dust; he lifts the needy from the ash heap, to make them sit with princes and inherit a seat of honor. For the pillars of the earth are the Lord's, and on them he has set the world.

1 Samuel 2:8 (NRSV)

Everything created by God is good, and nothing is to be rejected, provided it is received with thanksgiving; for it is sanctified by God's word and by prayer.

1 Timothy 4:4-5 (NRSV)

Time: Fifty minutes plus optional fifty minutes for supplemental activities

Materials:

- Leader's Guide
- Pens/pencils/scratch paper
- Overhead projector
- Overhead transparencies and handouts (optional)

Intention: To provide participants with an introduction to issues concerning the relationship between faith and global well-being

Objectives: During this session, participants will

1. Reflect on individual moral and spiritual responsibilities to others, one's community, and the world.
2. Explore issues of world poverty and hunger and reflect on appropriate Christian responses to these dilemmas.
3. Consider humanity's role as stewards of nature and discuss environmental issues that threaten global and local well-being.

Learning Activities

Setting Intention Through Reflection (five minutes)

- Introduce yourself briefly (if necessary). Briefly share your interest in the present topic.
- Welcome participants and encourage them to ask questions or contribute to discussions throughout the meetings.
- Summarize the accomplishments from previous sessions. The following paragraphs may be utilized for this purpose. Adapt them according to the activities completed.

> The first six sessions of this study guide have encouraged us to view health in relation to Christian faith; allowed us to explore the connection between our faith and our physical health; introduced us to the relationship between faith and mental health; helped us reflect on basic principles of the spiritual journey through deepening and expanding prayer; encouraged us to reflect on our communal life as a church and how it fosters both individual and congregational well-being; and allowed us to make the connection between faith and community service.
>
> Last time in Session 6, we became familiar with the Christian orientation toward addressing social problems, identified critical community-oriented social needs, and examined various opportunities for making a volunteer contribution.

- Ask for a moment of quiet and either offer a short prayer or invite a participant to offer one that sets an intention for participants to be open to learning and supporting each other. (See Activity 1 for suggested prayerful reflections.)

Introducing Activities Related to Session 7 (five minutes)

- Please read the following:

Today's activities broaden our focus from last time (faith and the well-being of society) by thinking of the entire world as one large community to which we belong. We will be exploring avenues through which we may play a positive part in sustaining the well-being of our world community.

- If you have chosen ahead of time one or two of the following activities for this session, read the appropriate descriptions (feel free to choose one of the supplemental activities as a main activity if you feel it best suits your group's needs).
- If you wish to allow time to let the group choose the activities for today's session, read the activity descriptions to introduce possible topics for exploration in today's lesson. Allow the group to choose one or two of the activities for completion during today's session.

Activity 2—Faith and Our Moral Responsibility (about fifteen to twenty minutes)
This activity encourages reflection on how our faith shapes our moral code and guides our actions. Furthermore, it allows participants to progressively reflect on moral obligations within relationships to others, our society, and the world.

Activity 3—Christian Responses to Global Poverty and Hunger (about fifteen to twenty minutes)
In this activity, we will explore the role that Christians can play in alleviating such global problems as poverty and hunger.

Activity 4—Environmental Stewardship: The Example of Noah (about fifteen to twenty minutes)
In this activity, we will reflect on the Genesis flood account and its interpretations and then examine the covenant that links human and nonhuman life with God as a way to approach current environmental issues.

Group Activities and Discussion (about thirty-five to forty minutes)

- Begin the chosen activity and conduct a group discussion. Prompts for group discussion are included in the activities in Questions to Consider.
- If time allows, begin the second chosen activity.

Concluding Reflections (five minutes)

- Ask participants for any concluding comments.
- Provide a summary and wrap-up of the meeting (see Summing Up).
- Thank participants and inquire into the group's interest in the optional supplemental activities (to work on either independently or at next meeting).

Supplemental, In-Group, or Take-Home Activities (fifty minutes)

Unexplored activities can be used as supplemental activities, allowing extended time for discussion or reflection.

You and/or participants can use Supplemental Activities A through C for resources within an extended meeting time or for independent learning. Supplemental Activity A provides an extension to Activity 2 (Faith and Moral Responsibility) by examining the moral code of our faith as outlined in a few pertinent principles. Supplemental Activity B explores the issue of war and the conditions under which it may be considered just. Finally, Supplemental Activity C provides an extension to Activity 4 (Environmental Stewardship: The Example of Noah) by offering numerous tips on environmental-friendly practices.

ACTIVITY 1:
SETTING INTENTION
THROUGH WELCOME AND PRAYER

Time: Five minutes

Objective: To welcome participants and to set an intention for learning

- Introduce yourself briefly, including your interest in the present topic.
- Welcome participants and encourage them to ask questions or contribute to discussions throughout the meetings.
- Ask for a moment of quiet and either offer a short prayer or invite a participant to offer one that sets an intention for participants to be open to learning and supporting each other. If you are interested in suggestions for an opening prayer, two such prayers are provided.

OPENING PRAYER
(Suggestion 1)

Holy Spirit,
giving life to all life,
moving all creatures,
root of all things,
washing them clean,
wiping out their mistakes,
healing their wounds,
you are our true life,
luminous, wonderful,
awakening the heart from its ancient sleep.

Hildegarde of Bingen, twelfth-century visionary,
healer, and author (http://www.worldprayers.org)

OPENING PRAYER
(Suggestion 2)

Blessed are the poor in spirit, for theirs is the kingdom of heaven.

Blessed are those who mourn, for they will be comforted.

Blessed are the meek, for they will inherit the earth.

Blessed are those who hunger and thirst for righteousness, for they will be filled.

Blessed are the merciful, for they will receive mercy.

Blessed are the pure in heart, for they will see God.

Blessed are the peacemakers, for they will be called children of God.

Blessed are those who are persecuted for righteousness' sake, for theirs is the kingdom of heaven.

Matthew 5:1-10 (NRSV)

ACTIVITY 2:
FAITH AND MORAL RESPONSIBILITY

Time: About fifteen to twenty minutes

Objective: To explore how our faith shapes our moral conduct

Our moral code has a strong influence on how we interact with and treat others. For the following activity, invite participants to pair up with another person in the room and share their answers to the questions offered on Overhead 7.1.

- Ask participants to select a partner to discuss the questions below.
- After everyone has discussed the above questions with a partner, reconvene the group. If you like, allow people to share some thoughts that arose in their discussion.
- Please read the following:

> The focus of this activity will now turn toward thinking of oneself as a citizen of a national or global community. There are certain responsibilities that come with being a citizen (e.g., paying taxes, voting, jury duty). In addition to these, one's faith will also serve to shape these moral responsibilities. Consequently, our faith will inherently influence the responsibilities we feel toward bettering the health and well-being of all people.

- Use Questions to Consider for Overhead 7.1 as prompts for discussion.

OVERHEAD 7.1. Questions regarding moral code.

---

1. In what ways does your moral code (ethics, moral principles, standards of right and wrong or justice and injustice) guide your behavior regarding the treatment of others? How has your faith influenced these values? Share some examples.

2. In what ways does your moral code guide your behavior regarding the treatment of others who are different from you (e.g., people with disabilities, different races)? How has your faith influenced these values? Share some examples.

3. In what ways does your moral code guide your behavior regarding others who are in need (e.g., living in poverty, suffering injustice)? How has your faith influenced these values? Share some examples.

Questions to Consider for Overhead 7.1

1. Drawing on your answers from earlier, what kind of moral responsibility do you feel toward helping others who are in need—especially when these others are people whom you've never met and will never meet?

2. The following is a quote from a Lutheran Church in America conference:

   Health is not just the health of a whole person but of the whole society. Health is a part of the mending of creation, but it must always be seen in the larger context of justice. There will never be health or the right distribution of health care in the world without justice. (Lutheran Church in America, n.d., p. 1)

   How does the idea of moral responsibility as a member of this nation and world relate to the quote's metaphor of health being "part of the mending of creation"?

3. How does the idea of moral responsibility relate to the idea of justice for all people in the world as described in the quote?

ACTIVITY 3:
"FOR I WAS HUNGRY AND YOU GAVE ME FOOD . . .":
CHRISTIAN RESPONSES TO GLOBAL POVERTY AND HUNGER

Time: About fifteen to twenty minutes

Objective: To examine the issues of global poverty and hunger and to explore Christian responses at the individual and congregational levels

- Choose volunteers to read the information offered on Overhead 7.2.
- Use Questions to Consider as prompts for discussion. Because these worldwide issues may seem too large to be affected by individuals at the local level, be sure to encourage participants to think about ways that they can make a difference during their daily lives and within their church and local communities.

OVERHEAD 7.2.
Poverty and hunger.

Poverty

· The wealthiest one-fifth of the world's people consume 86 percent of all goods and services, while the poorest one-fifth consumes 1 percent (United Nations Development Programme, *Human Development Report 1998*).
· Of the 6 billion people living in 2000, 1.2 billion live with less than $1 per day (World Bank, *World Development Report 2000/2001*).
· The amount of money that the richest 1 percent of the world's people makes each year equals what the poorest 57 percent make (United Nations Development Programme, *Human Development Report 2002*).
· Approximately 2.4 billion people lack access to basic sanitation, and 900 million people lack access to adequate health services (UNICEF, *State of the World's Children 2002*; United Nations Development Programme, *Human Development Report 1998*).

Hunger

· In developing countries, 91 children out of 1,000 die before their fifth birthday. By comparison, in the United States, 8 children in 1,000 will die before turning five years old (UNICEF, *The State of the World's Children 2000*).
· More than 800 million people in the world are malnourished—777 million of them are from the developing world (Food and Agriculture Organization of the United Nations, *The State of Food Insecurity in the World*, 2000; UNICEF, *The State of the World's Children 2001*).

- **Virtually every country in the world has the potential of growing sufficient food on a sustainable basis. The Food and Agriculture Organization of the United Nations has set the minimum requirement for caloric intake per person per day at 2,350. Fifty-four countries fall below that requirement. Most of these countries are in sub-Saharan Africa (Food and Agriculture Organization of the United Nations, *Mapping of the Food Supply Gap 1998*).**
- **Malnutrition can severely affect a child's intellectual development. Children who have stunted growth due to malnutrition score significantly lower on math and language achievement tests than do healthy children (UNICEF, *State of the World's Children 1998*).**

Questions to Consider

1. In Matthew 25, Jesus describes the actions of those who are blessed by God and will inherit eternal life. As he states, "For I was hungry and you gave me something to eat, I was thirsty and you gave me something to drink, I was a stranger and you invited me in." (25:35, NIV) How can this ethic of kindness and compassion be applied by Christians to address issues of world hunger and poverty?

2. In your experience, what steps can be taken at the individual, church, or local level to address issues of global poverty and hunger? What do you, your church, or your community currently do to confront these issues?

3. Have any of you ever witnessed the poverty of other nations? If so, what can you tell us about your experiences?

ACTIVITY 4:
ENVIRONMENTAL STEWARDSHIP:
THE EXAMPLE OF NOAH

Objective: To draw inspiration from the story of Noah in order to reflect on present environmental issues

- Ask participants to silently read Handout 7.1, about Noah and the flood account.
- Use Questions to Consider for Handout 7.1 as prompt for discussion.

HANDOUT 7.1. Noah and the flood.

According to Jewish rabbinical tradition, during the twelve months that Noah was on the Ark, he had no time to sleep. His restlessness, however, was not the product of the flood or his search for land. Instead, it is said that he was so busy tending to the needs of animals that there was no time for a break. In addition, the *Midrash* (a collection of Jewish commentaries on the Hebrew Scriptures written between 400 BC and AD 1200) cites a dialogue in which Abraham tells Noah and his sons that they survived the flood because of the faithfulness with which they cared for animals on the Ark.

Throughout Noah's journey he learned lessons of care and compassion, attention and responsibility. Wisdom and sympathy were nurtured within the Ark as its captain became a sustainer of life—a steward for God's creation.

As recounted in Genesis 9, God and Noah enter into a covenant after the rains ceased. God states, beginning in verse 12, "This is the sign of the covenant that I make between me and you and every living creature that is with you, for all future generations: I have set my bow in the clouds and it shall be a sign of the covenant between me and the earth. When I bring the clouds over the earth and the bow is seen in the clouds, I will remember my covenant that is between me and you and every living creature of all flesh; and the waters shall never again become a flood to destroy all flesh" (Genesis 9:12-15, NRSV).

Dr. J. Patrick Dobel, Professor of Public Affairs at the University of Washington, addressed notions of Christian stewardship of the earth's resources in the *Christian Century*. He wrote, "We must use the vast ethical and conceptual resources of the Judeo-Christian tradition to develop a God-centered ecological ethic which accounts for the sacredness of the earth without losing sight of human worth and justice" (1977, p. 906).

Questions to Consider for Handout 7.1

1. In your opinion, how should humans relate with other forms of life based on insights from the story of Noah and the covenant between God and creation?

2. Noah was a steward for all forms of life and carefully tended to the individual needs of the creatures in the Ark. How might his example be put to use in contemporary times (i.e., what are some major environmental crises and what responses might Christians offer to them)?

3. In your opinion, how can an improved environment facilitate social justice locally and globally?

4. What is the relationship between environmental problems and poverty, discrimination, or violence? How is the environment linked to local issues of health and justice?

SUMMING UP

Objective: To summarize what was learned in today's lesson

- You may use the following as guides for summarizing today's lesson:

> Today we explored various aspects of the well-being of society and the world we live in. Our explorations yielded a number of interesting insights.

- Choose whichever apply.

Faith and Moral Responsibility

> We reflected on how our faith informs our code of moral conduct. We then explored what influence our code of moral conduct might have on our role as a member of this nation and world. Our discussion revealed that. . . . [Use specific examples from the lesson.]

Christian Responses to Global Poverty and Hunger

> We briefly examined the issues of global poverty and hunger and then discussed what type of Christian response these issues call for. Some of our conclusions were. . . . [Use specific examples from the lesson.]

Environmental Stewardship: The Example of Noah

> We read information concerning the story of Noah and how he acted as a steward for the care of earth's animals. We then used this story as a source of inspiration regarding possible actions we may take to address current environmental problems. Some of our conclusions were. . . . [Use specific examples from the lesson.]

- Conclude with the following:

> Our explorations today were a brief introduction to the connection between Christian faith and national and global well-being. For those who have an interest in further exploration, feel free to examine the lesson(s) we were unable to attend to today. In addition, supplemental activities are provided as well.

- Note: Those who wish to explore any lessons independently will need copies of the directions from the Leader's Guide.

SUPPLEMENTAL ACTIVITY A:
FAITH AND THE MISSION OF HELPING

Time: About fifteen minutes

Objective: To explore how moral responsibility is outlined by one's faith tradition

- Display Overhead 7.3 and ask volunteers to read its paragraphs. (Note: If you have easy access to the Internet, you may want to review the principles outlined by your faith organization. A simple Internet search should bring up your faith tradition's homepage.)
- Use Questions to Consider for Overhead 7.3 as prompts for discussion.

OVERHEAD 7.3. Faith and the mission of helping.

Every faith tradition is actively involved in doing good works that help to contribute to society's health. In addition, each elaborates a set of principles that stem from their faith that then serve as a moral guide for their actions. The following example reflects a general statement of principles regarding social action as offered by the United Methodist Church (taken from the UMC Web site—www.umc.org).

The Natural World

All creation is the Lord's, and we are responsible for the ways we use and abuse it. Water, air, soil, minerals, energy resources, plants, animal life, and space are to be valued and conserved because they are God's creation and not solely because they are useful to human beings.

The Nurturing Community

The community provides the potential for nurturing human beings into the fullness of their humanity. We believe we have a responsibility to innovate, sponsor, and evaluate new forms of community that will encourage development of the fullest potential in individuals.

The Social Community

The rights and privileges a society bestows on or withholds from those who comprise it indicate the relative esteem in which that society holds particular persons and groups of persons. We affirm all persons as equally valuable in the sight of God.

The Economic Community

We claim all economic systems to be under the judgment of God no less than other facets of the created order.

The Political Community

While our allegiance to God takes precedence over our allegiance to any state, we acknowledge the vital function of government as a principal vehicle for the ordering of society. Because we know ourselves to be responsible to God for social and political life, we declare the following relative to governments: basic freedoms and human rights, political responsibility, freedom of information, education, civil obedience and civil disobedience, criminal and restorative justice.

The World Community

God's world is one world. We commit ourselves to the achievement of a world community that is a fellowship of persons who honestly love one another.

Questions to Consider for Overhead 7.3

1. In each of the categories highlighted in Overhead 7.3, what is the moral responsibility for social action involved in each principle?

2. In what ways do the statements compare with your own moral code (as was discussed in Activity 2)?

3. Please identify one or two actions to which you can commit that reflect a moral responsibility just identified and, thus, support the well-being of the world.

SUPPLEMENTAL ACTIVITY B:
WAR AND PEACE:
CHRISTIANITY'S JUST-WAR THEORY

Objective: To examine the issue of war and under what conditions war can be considered just

- Request that participants form small groups of three to four people.
- Distribute Handout 7.2 and ask participants to read the information. Then begin discussion of Small-Group Questions within their group.
- Reconvene the entire group to share insights from the discussions.

HANDOUT 7.2. War and peace: Christianity's just-war theory.

For 1,600 years, Christian theologians have attempted to answer the questions, "When is it permissible to wage war?" and "What should be the limitations of the ways we wage war?" These notions were originally addressed by Augustine in the fifth century AD when he claimed that war was a logical extension of the act of governance and that governments themselves were ordained by God. In the thirteenth century, Thomas Aquinas greatly expanded upon this theory in his *Summa Theologica*. There Aquinas wrote that for a war to be just it must be waged under the authority of a sovereign leader rather than a private individual; it must have a just cause; and it must have the intention of advancing good and avoiding evil. In the modern day, just-war theory is commonly said to consist of four parts derived from Augustine, Aquinas, and other Christian thinkers. These include

1. proper authority,
2. proper cause,
3. a reasonable chance of success, and
4. proportionality (that the harm caused by a response to aggression does not exceed the harm caused by the aggression itself).

Since the introduction of just-war theory by Augustine and Aquinas, many denominations have added to these principles within formal proclamations. For instance, the United Methodist Council of Bishops issued a statement in 1986 titled "In Defense of Creation." Here, the Council claimed that a just war must meet the following conditions:

1. just cause
2. just intent
3. last resort
4. legitimate authority
5. reasonable hope of success
6. discrimination
7. proportionality

Similarly, Roman Catholic bishops promulgated a statement in 1983 titled "The Challenge of Peace: God's Promise and Our Response." In the section labeled as "Jus ad Bellum," the bishops claimed that a just war must have the following:

1. just cause
2. competent authority
3. comparative justice
4. right intention
5. last resort
6. probability of success
7. proportionality

For more information, see United Methodist Council of Bishops. *In Defense of Creation: The Nuclear Crisis and a Just Peace.* Nashville, TN: Graded Press, 1986; National Conference of Catholic Bishops. *The Challenge of Peace: God's Promise and Our Response.* Washington, DC: United States Conference of Catholic Bishops, 1983; and Moseley, "Just war theory," http://www.iep.utm.edu/j/justwar.htm.

Small-Group Questions

1. Compare Christian principles for just war with the following biblical passage. Then discuss your views of whether war can be justified.

   Then they came and laid hands on Jesus and arrested him. Suddenly, one of those with Jesus put his hand on his sword, drew it, and struck the slave of the high priest, cutting off his ear. Then Jesus said to them, "Put your sword back in its place; for all who take the sword will perish by the sword." (Matthew 26:50-52 [NRSV])

2. How should Christian faith communities be involved in influencing the decision to wage war? Consider the following quote.

   If it is possible . . . live peaceably with all. Beloved, never avenge yourselves, but leave room for the wrath of God; for it is written, "Vengeance is mine, I will repay, says the Lord." (Romans 12:18-19 [NRSV])

3. Is it difficult for authorities to avoid "bearing the sword in vain"? If so, why? Consider the following quote.

   If you do what is wrong, you should be afraid, for the authority does not bear the sword in vain! It is the servant of God to execute wrath on the wrongdoer. (Romans 13:4 [NRSV])

4. What should be the ultimate aims or ends of a war?

5. In light of these considerations, what are the justice issues regarding the United States' current military approach to war?

SUPPLEMENTAL ACTIVITY C:
TAKING A HOME-BASED ECOLOGICAL INVENTORY

Objective: To learn more about various environmental-friendly practices.

- Allow participants a few minutes to quickly glance over Handout 7.3, which details environmental-friendly practices.
- Use Questions to Consider for Handout 7.3 to prompt discussion.

HANDOUT 7.3. Taking a home-based ecological inventory.

This handout contains a list of tips regarding numerous environment-friendly practices.

Reducing Toxic Chemical Use

Facts: Roughly 75,000 man-made chemicals are now in use. Many have not been adequately tested for the threats they may pose to human and nonhuman species (World Wildlife Fund, www.worldwildlife.org).

Reflections: What are the everyday chemicals that you use? How might they impact the environment after their use? What steps can be done to reduce the amounts you use?

How you can help:

- Look for the words "nontoxic" or "biodegradable" on the labels of products.
- Buy mercury-free rechargeable batteries; check with your local government for hazardous waste disposal sites.
- Grow disease- and pest-resistant plants.
- Use compost and mulch to improve soil health and reduce the need for pesticides and fertilizers.

Stopping Global Warming

Facts: Increasing evidence suggests that as pollution increases, so does the world's average temperature. Global warming forces rapid changes in human and animal habitats. Human industries and activities produce the world's air pollution, most of it carbon dioxide and other "greenhouse" gases that result in global warming. The United States releases approximately 40,000 pounds of carbon dioxide per person each year (World Wildlife Fund, www.worldwildlife.org).

Reflections: What daily activities in your own lives contribute to the release of "greenhouse" gases? How might you take steps to reduce these amounts?

How you can help:

- Buy a car that gets at least thirty miles to the gallon. This reduces carbon dioxide 2,500 pounds per year more than a car that gets twenty miles per gallon.
- Replace standard light bulbs with energy-efficient flourescents. This reduces emissions by 500 pounds per year per light bulb.
- Wrap your water heater in an insulating jacket. This reduces emissions up to 1,000 pounds per year.
- Install low-flow showerheads that use less water. This reduces emissions up to 300 pounds per year.

Protecting Forests

Facts: Forests stand as great storehouses of natural life. However, nearly two-thirds of the world's original forests are gone. Forests fall to the chainsaw at an accelerating pace driven by an international timber trade (World Wildlife Fund, www.worldwildlife.org).

Reflections: How can you protect forests during your everyday lives? What daily activities contribute to the depletion of forests?

How you can help:

- Use electronic communications and nonpaper learning resources.
- Buy recycled paper products.
- Use and promote convenient and practical paper recycling.
- Buy firewood from "downed wood" sources.
- Purchase wood products certified by the Forest Stewardship Council (FSC). You can find information about these products at www.fscus.org. Ask your home builder, remodeler, or architect to use FSC-certified products. Inquire with your local building materials retailer about products that are FSC certified.

Saving Water

Facts: Water is a precious resource in our environment. Growing populations and ongoing droughts are squeezing our water resources dry, causing natural habitat degradation and impacting our everyday use of water. On average, Americans use 150 gallons of water per person per day (Earth 911, www.earth911.org).

Reflections: Do you think about your daily water use? If so, what steps do you take to reduce water consumption while at home? What might be the chief sources of water consumption in your household?

How you can help:

- Check for toilet leaks by adding food coloring to the tank. If the toilet is leaking, color will appear in the bowl within thirty minutes. Avoid unnecessary flushing. Dispose of tissues, insects, and other similar waste in the trash rather than the toilet.
- Take shorter showers. Do not let the water run while shaving, washing your face, or brushing your teeth.
- Minimize the use of kitchen sink disposals; they require a lot of water to operate properly. Start a compost pile as an alternate method of disposing of food waste.
- Don't overwater your lawn. As a general rule, lawns need watering only every five to seven days in the summer. A hearty rain eliminates the need for watering for as long as two weeks. Do not leave sprinklers or hoses unattended. Your garden hose can pour out 600 gallons or more in only a few hours. Use a kitchen timer to remind yourself to turn the water off.
- Raise your lawn mower blade to at least three inches. A lawn cut higher encourages grass roots to grow deeper, shades the root system, and holds soil moisture better than closely clipped lawns.

Lessening Consumer Impact Through Reducing and Reusing

Facts: In 1998, Americans generated 220 million tons of garbage—an increase of 4 million tons over the previous year. This equates to approximately 4.46 pounds per person, per day (Waste Management, Inc., http://www.mn-wastesolutions.com).

Reflections: How could you reduce the amount of trash that you send to the landfill? What items do you put out for the trash that could be reused or recycled?

How you can help:

- Reduce the volume of packaging you buy, and reuse what you can.
- Buy quality products and keep them for a lifetime.

Lessening Consumer Impact Through Recycling

Facts: Enough aluminum is thrown away to rebuild America's commercial air fleet four times every year. Glass can be reused an infinite number of times, and, according to the Environmental Protection Agency (EPA), over 41 billion glass containers are made each year. Every year enough paper is thrown away to make a twelve-foot-high wall from New York to California. According to the EPA, Americans use enough plastic wrap to wrap all of Texas every year. According to the Steel Recycling Institute, enough iron and steel is discarded in the United States to continually supply the nation's automakers (Office of Waste Management, University of Massachusetts–Amherst, http://www.umass.edu/recycle/index.html).

Reflections: Do you recycle? If so, what types of materials? If not, why? Is there a recycling center close to your home? Does your city have a curbside recycling program? What steps can you take to either increase the amount of materials you recycle or begin a recycling "habit"?

How you can help:

- *Aluminum* is easy to recognize and recycle. Clean aluminum containers only with enough water to prevent odors. The high temperature of processing deals easily with contamination caused by leftover foods or liquids.
- All colors of *glass* are recyclable. Glass bottles must not be mixed with other types of glass, such as windows, light bulbs, mirrors, glass tableware, Pyrex, or auto glass.
- Most types of *paper* can be recycled. The key to recycling is collecting large quantities of clean, well-sorted, uncontaminated, and dry paper. The entire newspaper, including inserts, is acceptable, except accompanying plastic, product samples, and rubber bands.
- *Plastic* recycling faces one huge problem: plastic types must not be mixed for recycling, yet it is impossible to tell one type from another by sight or touch. The plastic industry has responded to this problem by developing a series of markers commonly placed on the bottom of plastic containers. You should put in your bin *only* those types of plastic listed by your local recycling agency.
- Recycle everything that your local recycling center accepts.

Questions to Consider for Handout 7.3

1. What environmental-friendly practices do you currently follow?

2. What motivated you to adopt these practices? (Does it connect to the earlier activity of environmental stewardship?) Please elaborate.

3. Of the tips you have just glanced over, what if any new practices captured your attention and interest? Please elaborate.

Session 8

The End Is Just the Beginning

Tomb, St. Louis Cemetery #1, New Orleans, Louisiana.

By the tender mercy of our God, the dawn from on high will break upon us, to give light to those who sit in darkness and in the shadow of death, to guide our feet into the way of peace.

Luke 1:78-79 (NRSV)

He was praying in a certain place, and after he had finished, one of his disciples said to him, "Lord, teach us to pray, as John taught his disciples." He said to them, when you pray, say:
> *Father, hallowed be your name.*
> *Your kingdom come.*
> *Give us each day our daily bread.*
> *And forgive us our sins, for we ourselves forgive everyone indebted to us.*
> *And do not bring us to the time of trial.*

Luke 11:1-4 (NRSV)

Health Through Faith and Community
Published by The Haworth Press, Inc., 2006. All rights reserved.
doi:10.1300/5595_09

Time: Fifty minutes plus optional fifty minutes for supplemental activities

Materials:

- Leader's Guide
- Pens/pencils/scratch paper
- Overhead projector
- Overhead transparencies and handouts
- Chalk and chalkboard (Activity 2)
- Pieces of colored cardstock cut into rectangular-shaped bookmarks (Activity 3)

Purpose: To process and reflect on what has been learned during the previous sessions and to set priorities for the future

Objectives: During this session, participants will

1. Articulate and clarify key insights learned in the previous sessions.
2. Build a personal and group agenda for future actions stemming from key insights.
3. Commit to individual and group actions for the future.
4. Seek to bring personal and group closure to the course.

Learning Activities

Setting Intention Through Reflection (five minutes)

- Introduce yourself briefly, if necessary and relate to participants that this will be the final session (unless follow-up activities are desired).
- Welcome participants, and encourage them to ask questions or contribute to discussions throughout the meeting.
- Summarize the accomplishments from previous sessions. The following paragraphs may be utilized for this purpose. Adapt them according to the activities completed.

> We are near completion of our journey together. The seven sessions of this study guide have encouraged us to view health as related to Christian faith; allowed us to explore the connection between our faith and our physical health; introduced us to the relationship between faith and mental health; helped us reflect on basic principles of the spiritual journey through deepening and expanding prayer; encouraged us to reflect on our communal life as a church and how it fosters both individual and congregational well-being; allowed us to make the connection between faith and community service; and introduced us to the relationship between faith and national or global well-being.
>
> Last time in Session 7, we reflected on individual moral responsibilities to others, one's community, one's nation, and the planet. We discussed issues of poverty, hunger, and the environment that threaten global well-being.

- Ask for a moment of quiet and either offer a short prayer or invite a participant to offer one that sets an intention for participants to be open to learning and supporting each other. (See Activity 1 for suggested prayerful reflections.)

Introducing Activities for Session 8 (five minutes)

- Please read the following:

> Today's activities focus on both a look backward and a look forward. We look backward in order to one last time share our key insights over these past seven sessions. We also look forward to how we might incorporate these insights as a regular part of our daily lives.

- Read the following activity descriptions to introduce the topics to explore in today's session.
- Inform the group that today you will be doing these activities in order.

> *Activity 2—Sharing Key Insights (twenty minutes)*
> In this activity, we will be looking back at the seven sessions that we have explored. Participants will be asked to share ideas and impressions that particularly struck home with them from whichever sessions they could attend.

> *Activity 3—Concluding Ritual (twenty minutes)*
> In this activity, we will display appreciation for the participation and support shown by everyone over the course of the sessions. We will also seek to put our newly gained insights into action by creating goals to improve both personal and community levels of health.

Group Activities and Discussion/Sharing (forty minutes)

- Begin Activity 2 and conduct a group discussion. Prompts for group discussion are included in Questions to Consider for Activity 2.
- Conclude with Activity 3.

Concluding Reflections (five minutes)

- Ask participants for any concluding comments.
- Provide a summary and wrap-up of the meeting (see Summing Up).
- Thank participants and inquire into the group's interest in the optional supplemental activities, including the possibility of forming a group to plan for continued congregational efforts to promote personal and community health.

Supplemental, In-Group, or Take-Home Activities (fifty minutes)

Unexplored activities from Sessions 1 through 7 can be used as supplemental activities, allowing extended time for discussion or reflection.

The End is Just the Beginning: Creating Further Faith Community Initiatives

Although the last study session has been concluded, this can be just the beginning of ongoing and expanding activities. If you discover that there is major interest and enthusiasm in the congregation to promote personal and social well-being, you should consider establishing an Action Committee to plan and implement initiatives. (See the Summing Up section at the end of this session.) We offer guidelines for creating and conducting such a committee on our Web site: http://www.healthfaithstudy.info/. This Web site is for the online Spiritual Diversity and Social Work Resource Center that was created as a complement and expansion of this study guide. It provides numerous bibliographical resources, essays, internet links, and a photo gallery that address connections between spirituality, health, and social service in Christian and other religious traditions. See the link for Action Committee Guide.

ACTIVITY 1:
SETTING INTENTION
THROUGH WELCOME AND PRAYER

Time: Five minutes

Objective: To welcome participants and to set an intention for learning.

- Introduce yourself briefly, including your interest in the present topic.
- Welcome participants and encourage them to ask questions or contribute to discussions throughout the meetings.
- Ask for a moment of quiet and either offer a short prayer or invite a participant to offer one that sets an intention for participants to be open to learning and supporting each other. If you are interested in a suggestion for an opening prayer, two such prayers are provided.

OPENING PRAYER
(Suggestion 1)

**God is our refuge and our strength,
a very present help in trouble.
Therefore we will not fear, though
the earth should change,
though the mountains shake in the
heart of the sea;
though its waters roar and foam,
though the mountains tremble
with its tumult.**

Psalm 46:1-3 (NRSV)

OPENING PRAYER
(Suggestion 2)

Make a joyful noise to the Lord, all
the earth.
Worship the Lord with gladness;
come into his presence with singing.

Know that the Lord is God.
it is he that made us, and we are
his;
we are his people, and the sheep
of his pasture.

Enter his gates with thanksgiving,
and his courts with praise,
Give thanks to him, bless his name.

For the Lord is good;
his steadfast love endures forever,
And his faithfulness to all
generations.

Psalm 100 (NRSV)

ACTIVITY 2:
SHARING KEY INSIGHTS FROM THE SESSIONS

Time: Twenty minutes

Objective: To reflect on lessons learned and share what has struck you the most

- Please read the following:

> Over the course of the past seven sessions, we have hopefully expanded our ideas about personal and social health. Take a few minutes to reflect on these past sessions. Write down any key insights or ideas from the activities that have left a lasting impression from any sessions that you were able to attend. We will then share these with each other.

Session 1: Holistic Christian approach to health and well-being; faith and health; Jesus as healer

Session 2: Meaning through suffering; faith and physical health

Session 3: Faith and mental health; using proverbs for insight; symbolism of the cross

Session 4: Dimensions of faith development; prayer and spirituality

Session 5: Healthy congregational relationships; leadership; role structures within the church

Session 6: Faith-based community organizing; faith and service to society

Session 7: Moral responsibility; global hunger and poverty; environmental stewardship

- During the discussion that follows, write down insights shared by participants on a chalkboard or overhead. Invite participants to write down any new insights (Question 2) that they learn from others.
- Discuss the similarities and differences among the various insights from the group.

As a result of this process, participants may hopefully gain some new insights about personal and social health. Also, this activity is geared toward solidifying insights already gained.

Questions to Consider for Activity 2

1. Write down any insights that you have gained as a result of your time in this course. Try to include at least one insight about yourself and one insight about some aspect of the community (congregation, neighborhood, nation, world, etc.).

2. As a result of everyone sharing their insights from question 1, what did you learn from the insights of others?

ACTIVITY 3:
CONCLUDING RITUAL

Time: Twenty minutes

Objective: To encourage each participant to commit to one individual action and to one group action

- Please read the following:

> Now that we have shared our insights, this last activity looks toward what we will take away with us from these sessions by setting some future goals. Please reflect a few minutes on one faith-influenced action that can improve your personal health. Do the same for one faith-influenced action that can improve the health of the local community, nation, or world.

- After participants have had adequate time to reflect, adapt the suggestions below for a concluding ritual.

Suggestions for Concluding Ritual

- On two pieces of colored cardstock in the shape of bookmarks, ask each person to write his or her individual action (e.g., pray for well-being of loved ones and the world) on one bookmark and his or her group action (e.g., join a community action project; start a church recycling program) on the other bookmark.
- Then, ask everyone to stand or sit in a circle.
- Taking turns, direct each person to read his or her group action aloud or silently (either one is fine).
- Taking turns, direct each person to read his or her individual action aloud or silently (either one is fine).
- The group should listen with respect to each person. If a member reads the action silently, all should sit together in respectful quiet. At the end, the group can clap for each other as a way to express appreciation and encouragement.
- Lead a brief prayer of thanks and for guidance as a way to acknowledge the conclusion of the ritual and the course and in optimism for the future.
- Encourage everyone to keep his or her bookmarks until the action on it has been completed. Then the person privately can burn the bookmark or save it in a special place while offering a prayer of reflection and thanks.

SUMMING UP

Objective: To thank participants for their commitment to learning

- Say a few brief words thanking participants for their attendance and participation.
- You may use the following, if appropriate:

Before we all leave, I just wanted to thank you all for your attendance and participation during these sessions. Not only have you helped make this an enjoyable experience, but your commitment bodes well for maintaining your personal well-being and for attending to the health of our community—at all its various levels.

- You may also add the following:

In addition, if any of you are interested in planning further activities that support personal and social well-being, please let me know. We could work with other members of our congregation to develop an action committee that would plan and implement these activities on an ongoing basis. Please let me know if you are interested.

References

Session 1

Canda, E. R., (2001). Transcending through disability and death: Transpersonal themes in living with cystic fibrosis. In E. R. Canda & E. D. Smith (Eds.), *Transpersonal perspectives on spirituality in social work* (pp. 109-134). Binghamton, NY: The Haworth Press.

Canda, E. R. (2002). The significance of spirituality for resilient response to chronic illness: A qualitative study of adults with cystic fibrosis. In Saleebey, D. (Ed.), *The strengths perspective in social work practice* (third edition, pp. 63-79). Boston: Allyn and Bacon.

Kelsey, M. (1987). *Encounter with God.* New York: Paulist Press.

Session 2

Canda, E. C. (2001). Transcending through disability and death: Transpersonal themes in living with cystic fibrosis. In E. Canda & E. Smith (Eds.), *Transpersonal perspectives on spirituality in social work* (pp. 109-134). Binghamton, NY: The Haworth Press.

Hummer, R. A., Rogers, R. G., Nam, C. B., & Ellison, C. G. (1999). Religious involvement and U.S. adult mortality. *Demography, 36*(2), 1-13.

Koenig, H. G. et al. (1998). The relationship between religious activities and blood pressure in older adults. *International Journal of Psychology in Medicine, 28*(2), 189-213.

McBride, J. L., Arthur, G., Brooks, R., & Pilkington, L. (1998). The relationship between a patient's spirituality and health experiences. *Family Medicine, 30*(2), 122-126.

Wagner, J. K. (1993). *An adventure in healing and wholeness: The healing ministry of Christ in the church today.* Nashville: Upper Room.

Session 3

Keller, J. E. (1985). *Let go, let God.* Minneapolis: Augsburg Publishing House.

Koenig, H. G., George, L. K, & Peterson, B. L. (1998). Religiosity and remission of depression in medically ill older adults. *American Journal of Psychiatry, 155*(4), 536-542.

Koenig, H. G., McCullough, M. E., & Larson, D. B. (2001). *Handbook of religion and health.* Oxford: Oxford University Press.

Miller, W. R. (1998). Researching the spiritual dimensions of alcohol and other drug problems. *Addiction, 93*(7), 979-990.

Shifrin, J. (1999). *Pathways to understanding: A manual on ministry and mental illness.* St. Louis, MO: Pathways to Promise.

Shifrin, J. (Ed.) (n.d.). *Caring congregations: Observations and commentary.* St. Louis, MO: Pathways to Promise.

Williams, R. W., Larson, D. B., Buckler, R. E., Heckmann, R. C., & Pyle, C. M. (1991). Religion and psychological distress in a community sample. *Social Science Medicine, 32*(11), 1257-1262.

Session 4

Canda, E. R., & Furman, L. D. (1999). *Spiritual diversity in social work practice.* New York: The Free Press.

Fowler, J. (1991). *Weaving the new creation.* San Francisco: HarperSanFancisco.

Fowler, J. (2000). *Becoming adult, becoming Christian.* San Francisco: Jossey-Bass Publishers.

Health Through Faith and Community
Published by The Haworth Press, Inc., 2006. All rights reserved.
doi:10.1300/5595_10

Hastings, A. (2000). "Prayer." *The Oxford companion to Christian thought* (pp. 555-556). New York: Oxford University Press.

Keating, T. (1994). *Invitation to love: The way of Christian contemplation.* New York: Continuum Publishing Group.

Keating, T. (2002). *Foundations for centering prayer and the Christian contemplative life: Open mind, open heart, invitation to love, mystery of Christ.* New York: Continuum Publishing Group.

Kempis, T. à. (1989). *The imitation of Christ.* William C. Creasy (Trans.). Macon, GA: Mercer University Press.

New Catholic encyclopedia. (2003). "Thomas à Kempis." Washington, DC: Catholic University of America.

Rahner, K. (1975). "Prayer." *Encyclopedia of theology* (pp. 1268-1277). New York: The Seabury Press.

Session 5

Carson, V. B., & Koenig, H. G. (2002). *Parish nursing: Stories of service and care.* Philadelphia: Templeton Foundation Press.

Evans, J. (1992). *We have been believers.* Minneapolis: Fortress Press.

Lee, D. (1991). Bridging the gap between clergy and laity. *Spirituality and Social Work Communicator, 2*(1), 5-7.

Whitehead, J. D., & Whitehead, E. E. (1986). *The emerging laity: Returning leadership to the community of faith.* Garden City, NY: Doubleday and Company.

Session 6

Book of discipline of the United Methodist Church—2000. (2000). "The Economic Community." Nashville: United Methodist Publishing House.

National Center for Health Statistics. (2002). *Health, United States, 2002.* Hyattsville, MD: U.S. Department of Health and Human Services, Centers for Disease Control and Prevention, National Center for Health Statistics, Division of Data Services.

Tarlov, A. R., and St. Peter, R. F. (Eds.) (2000). *The society and population health reader: A state and community perspective.* New York: The New Press.

Session 7

Dobel, J. P. (1977). Stewards of the earth's resources: A Christian response to ecology. *Christian Century,* October 12, 906+.

Food and Agriculture Organization of the United Nations. (1998). *Mapping of the food supply gap 1998.* Oxford: Oxford University Press.

Food and Agriculture Organization of the United Nations. (2000). *The state of food insecurity in the world.* Oxford: Oxford University Press.

Lutheran Church of Australia. (n.d.). Conference on health, healing, and health care. Findings: The LCA Conference on health, healing and health care (New York, n.d.), as quoted in: Numbers, Ronald Lo & Amundsen, Darrel W. (Eds.), (1986). *Caring and curing: Health and Medicine in the Western religious traditions* (p. 198). Baltimore, MD: The Johns Hopkins University Press.

Mosley, A. (n.d.) Just war theory. *The Internet encyclopedia of philosophy.* Available at http://www.iep.utm.edu/j/justwar.htm.

UNICEF. (2000). *The state of the world's children 2000.* New York: UNICEF Publications.

UNICEF. (2001). *The state of the world's children 2001.* New York: UNICEF Publications.

UNICEF. (2002). *The state of the world's children 2002.* New York: UNICEF Publications.

United Nations Development Programme. (1998). *Human development report 1998.* Oxford: Oxford University Press.

United Nations Development Programme. (2002). *Human development report 2002.* Oxford: Oxford University Press.

World Bank. (2000). *World development report 2000/2001: Attacking poverty.* Oxford: Oxford University Press.

Index

Page numbers followed by the letter "b" indicate boxed material; those followed by the letter "i" indicate illustrations.

Health Through Faith and Community
Published by The Haworth Press, Inc., 2006. All rights reserved.
doi:10.1300/5595_11